REFINED

REFINED

A MEMOIR

TRACIE BREAUX

DEACON & ROTH PUBLISHING GROUP
NEW YORK

Refined is a work of nonfiction. Some names and identifying details have been changed.

Copyright © 2022 by Tracie Breaux

All rights reserved.

Published in the United States by Deacon & Roth, New York.

LIBRARY OF CONGRESS CATALOGING-IN-PUBLICATION DATA
NAMES: Breaux, Tracie, author.
TITLE: Refined: a memoir / Tracie Breaux.
DESCRIPTION: New York : Deacon & Roth, [2022]
IDENTIFIERS: ISBN 9781737713708 |
ISBN 9781737713222 (ebook)
Library of Congress Control Number: 2022901232.
SUBJECTS: LCSH: Breaux, Tracie—Family. | Women—Louisiana—Biography. | Family Violence—Louisiana—Biography. | Child Abuse—Louisiana—Anecdotes. | Women entrepreneurs—United States—Biography. |

traciebreaux.com

Book design by Patrick Svensson, adapted for ebook

Cover illustration: Patrik Svensson

Forgiving does not erase the bitter past. A healed memory is not a deleted memory. Instead, forgiving what we cannot forget creates a new way to remember. We change the memory of our past into a hope for our future.

— LEWIS B. SMEDES

Hope sees the invisible, feels the intangible, and achieves the impossible.

— HELEN KELLER

CONTENTS

Author's Note i
Prologue 1
PART ONE 3
    Chapter 1: Watch Mom at Work 5
    Chapter 2: Twilight Zone 11
    Chapter 3: Promised Land 15
    Chapter 4: Wind Horse 21
    Chapter 5: Video Game 26
    Chapter 6: Rat Jabber 35
    Chapter 7: Adopted 40
    Chapter 8: The Battlefield 46
    Chapter 9: Lion 53
    Chapter 10: Operation Great Escape 63
    Chapter 11: Winds of Change 67
PART TWO 75
    Chapter 12: Copious Power 77
    Chapter 13: Sisters 89
    Chapter 14: Molly 102
    Chapter 15: The Prize and the Pain 111
    Chapter 16: The Dungeon 118
    Chapter 17: The Mooring Rope 127
    Chapter 18: Frontier 140
PART THREE 149
    Chapter 19: The Circus 151
    Chapter 20: Moving Out 158
    Chapter 21: The Fractured Daughter 168
    Chapter 22: Me Too 178
    Chapter 23: Refined 191
ABOUT THE AUTHOR 204

AUTHOR'S NOTE

This is not a religious book. Various religions are used throughout to continue the story. The author believes that each person is responsible for his or her walk in life, whether affiliated with a religious organization or not. The author does not believe that any religion is better or worse than the other. At the end of the day, each of us is responsible for who we are.

Identifying details have been changed in the book for living persons. Pseudonyms have been used for all living individuals. The names Avis, Travis, and Carol are real names. All three persons are deceased.

PROLOGUE

I was running through a black forest.

A great rush of wind whipped my hair behind me as I flew down the trail lit by a full moon. Limbs brushed against me, as if the trees themselves were patting my arms. Behind me, the footpath was intense, and thundering, as two men pursued me.

Blood pulsed through my head so fast it was like a wrecking ball banging around in my skull. Moments before, I'd been huddled in a small clearing, folding myself against a tree when twigs snapped.

"Quiet! She's going to hear us," a voice said. Then, "Do you have the rope?"

I grabbed my bag and bolted.

I was a fifteen-year-old runaway, but I wasn't just running from the men who'd seen me enter the trees earlier. For the last few years, I had been running from everyone and everything, but mostly I was running from my father, Frankie. Every year of my life, I watched in horror as he folded and snapped my mother's bones and I gagged as she spit streams of blood into the sink. Most report card days, he put crimson stripes, speckled like a robin's egg, on my younger brother Bubba's thighs. He smashed Bubba into drywall when he was ten years old. Dad kept us in an around-the-clock state of terror, waiting for a trigger to click and set him off. Because he was unhappy with himself, we suffered.

I'd starting scheming how to leave home about a year before, after I watched a movie on television starring Steve McQueen. *The Great Escape* became the name of my plan. The night before, my idea had been set into motion when Dad charged into my room threatening me. I got up the next morning and left for good. Left the beatings and screams. Left the fear and hopelessness. Leaving home felt like the weight of the world had floated off my shoulders. However, just before dusk, two men shifted their truck in reverse and watched me walk a worn path into the black forest. I don't know if they left and came back or waited in the shadows until the sun disappeared on the other side of the planet. All I know is after the light was gone, they were chasing me. With a rope.

It was while I was running in the forest, I believed I wouldn't make it out, that my fate was sealed inside its blackness, and the fire in my bones that had kept me surviving all my years would ebb out like the last flicker of a candle. No one would ever know what happened to me.

Trailing me, one of the men shouted, "Grab her!"

I spied a narrow bayou ahead. Beams of moonlight shone down from the inky sky and illuminated the water, which gleamed like a chalky ribbon weaving across the ground. As I ran toward it, I studied the eight-foot-wide chasm.

I wasn't sure if I could make it across. Twigs cracked and popped behind me. They were gaining on me. A scream from one of the men echoed, like the bloodcurdling screech of a barn owl. The other man shouted, "SNAKE!" as I neared the water. *I can do this*, I chanted, and without looking back, I arched my body and leapt.

PART ONE

Chapter 1:

Watch Mom at Work

—

My book of memories is not an actual book. It's something that came about when I asked my mom's aunt Carol how she remembered everything in such detail, even passages and their page numbers from books she'd read decades earlier. She was the smartest person I knew.

Aunt Carol was about six-feet tall with auburn hair and glasses so thick the lenses looked like the bottoms of soda pop bottles. Her eyesight was bad; if she wasn't wearing the glasses, she couldn't tell the difference between a bus and a person dressed in yellow. Numerous books were displayed in different areas of the home she and Grandma Avis shared. A book could usually be found splayed between the spindly fingers on her left hand, a glass of iced tea in her right.

She slid a plate of cookies on the table and poured me a glass of milk, then sat on the chair next to me. As I stuffed cookies into my mouth, she told me a story of her brother, Travis, my grandmother's twin. I could hear Grandma Avis behind me shifting on a stool. Because she had polio as a child, she had trouble sitting on anything else. She always got quiet when his name was brought up.

Aunt Carol told me most days, when Travis was a teenager, he'd stomp out the door with either a baseball bat slung over his shoulder, or a football tucked under his arm. But boxing was his first love. He'd gone out of town for a match during his junior year of high school when she saw him last.

"I was fourteen years old," she continued. "Travis was seventeen. I wasn't there to tell him bye. The next time I saw him, he was in a wood box."

Her German shepherd, Butch, nudged her. She slipped him a cookie, then continued.

"A few years later, I thought about what my last words were to him, but as hard as I tried, I couldn't remember."

I'd once seen a black-and-white photograph of Travis. He was lean and muscular, like an athlete. I imagined him loping out the door, boxing gloves tucked under his arm, for the final time. I pictured my great-aunt Carol beating herself up because she couldn't remember the last words she said to him. She told me ever since his death, she had tried to focus on an object, then recited, "I want to remember this moment for the rest of my life."

"Did you make a memory today?" I asked.

"Yes, I did." She took a long sip of iced tea and stared at Butch, who was nudging her for another cookie.

"I'm going to make a memory too," I said, staring hard into the empty plate. "I'll remember this for the rest of my life."

After Aunt Carol taught me how to make memories, I jammed my brain with them. Soon after, my parents packed all our things and moved us from north Louisiana.

About a year later, I was studying a handful of burly men in steel-toed boots and hard hats from the shadows of an oil refinery in southern Arkansas. Their muscles ballooned under the fabric of their shirts as they strained to hoist a steel pipe onto a truck. Minutes before, I had fled from home, racing the few blocks to the refinery after my father became enraged when he saw a man walking on our street.

At seven years old, I wondered if the men hoisting the pipe were the villains my dad was so afraid of. Mom and Dad were always arguing, sometimes about money, but mostly about men. He often screamed at her about how they followed Mom home or how he caught one gawking at her. Dad would return from work and peek in the closets or under a bed hoping to catch one, but he never did. He was so sure that somehow they eluded him, that he'd stand on the front porch, a lit cigarette hanging from his lip, his eyes sweeping the neighborhood for one who might have fled. Eventually, he'd huff back inside and holler at Mom about how lucky she was he hadn't caught a man.

The villains didn't exist, of course—like The Joker or The Mad Hatter—but the way my father's neck bulged as he searched the neighborhood for one made me believe they were lurking everywhere, hunting for us.

Standing between the rails of a spur line, I wasn't quite old enough to know that beneath my feet were lakes of liquid gold and the men who trudged in and out of the refinery weren't scoundrels at all. I didn't know people could live in harmony together without punching holes in the walls, kicking the dog, or smashing the television.

My father was twenty-four years old with a boyish face, golden hair, and eyes so blue they made you want to swim in them. Rough and rebellious, he limited our time with his parents and siblings. I also didn't know that the darkness associated in our family had a haunting history of trauma passed down for perhaps hundreds of years, a past rich in petty crimes, theft, and murder. I didn't know that my ancestors, each who'd set out to free themselves of the generation before them, would leave behind their own ancient fragments along the way.

I didn't understand a lot of things, but the one thing I did was this: my dad's obsession with other men was not normal. His greatest fear was that someone would take my mother away from him. We couldn't open the windows in our home because he'd nailed them shut to keep men from crawling in. We couldn't look out because Dad had tacked multiple layers of trash bags across the frames so no one could see us. The kids at school nicknamed me Trash Bag Tracie and tossed pieces of trash at me. I spent my days dodging balls of notebook paper and used candy wrappers. There were evenings I wanted to rip the bags off, just to be rid of them, but my fear of Dad's rage was too great.

Daily my mother had to prove her trustworthiness to him. We *all* had to prove our loyalty, including my six-year-old brother. My father trained me to sit outside the bathroom when Mom went in, my ear pressed against the door—listening to her pee—mentally timing her movements. If I heard the window being tampered with, I was to report this information back to Dad. It never was.

Staring at the refinery, I imagined it was something magical that could transport me to a different world. It's this mental snapshot that I cataloged in my book of memories, the polished columns pointing up to the heavens like spires, rockets—bathed in a soft amber light—pulsating like living things. The refinery was a beacon of hope, of possibility.

I looked back at the men who were lifting more pipes, beads of sweat falling from their foreheads onto the ground. *They don't look like villains*, I thought, gazing across the shiny tract of land. My dad's fears frightened me so much I wanted to uncork my strength and run as far away as I could from him.

My entire childhood was centered around my father's paranoias—his fixation on other men, his obsession with my mother, his dependence on being the center of our tiny family's universe. I knew I wanted out of my father's world of violence and delusions of men, to a place where I would feel safe and empowered. I just didn't know at the time that a set of rails would lead me there.

———

MY MOTHER, LINDA, WAS twenty-five years old and the most beautiful woman I ever saw. She had long silky hair, a cascade the color of midnight, and dusky brown eyes that made your heart melt, even if you didn't want it to. She had a Singer sewing machine in the living room next to a small basket of fabric scraps. When Mom wasn't reading, she was hunched over the machine on a small wooden chair, with a pin cushion that looked like a tomato strapped to her wrist, sewing clothes for us, or patching the knees of Bubba's jeans. Most days she put on a burgundy uniform with white stripes at the collar to work at McDonald's.

Sometimes Dad brought Bubba and me to her job to eat hamburgers and play a game called Watch Mom at Work. He hovered near the counter, staring at the menu, acting as though he didn't have it memorized, then his eyes would shift to Mom. He'd stand for several minutes, taking deep, choppy breaths, gazing at her as she checked customers at the register.

One chilly Saturday, my father seemed extra breathless, agitated. He paced the house for a while, mumbling to himself about men. The men, I understood, could not be trusted. Eventually, he hoisted Bubba and me into his pickup. The three of us skidded onto the highway, headed to McDonald's. When we arrived, he circled the block again and again, scanning for men who might have fled the restaurant. Dad pulled into an empty space and slammed on the brakes. He shifted the truck in park, then rushed out the driver's seat and charged inside the building. Bubba and I scrambled behind.

Dad appraised the inside of the restaurant. Mom was nowhere to be seen. He shuffled around the registers, eyes flashing, panting. The ceramic Ronald McDonald looked nervous.

As I slid past Ronald McDonald, I caught sight of Mom leaving a restroom. I tugged on the hem of Dad's shirt and pointed.

"One day I'll catch her," he muttered.

We ate our hamburgers in silence. Dad watched to make sure male customers didn't hover too long while paying for their burgers. After we ate, Bubba and I played on the outdoor playground. We were always playing Watch Mom at Work, but it wasn't a fun game, and I think the only person who won was Dad.

I COULDN'T HELP HER.

It was evening. Dad was in a mood. Mom was a few minutes late coming home from work. He stared blankly at the flickering television. He told me to fetch him a beer. After I returned with the beer, he glanced in the direction of the clock. I sat on the floor to play a game with Bubba.

When he heard the lock to the back door click, then the knob twist, Dad leaped up from the recliner. His steel-toed boots smashed dolls and diecast cars before he jumped the sofa and lunged for the opening of the door. Mom appeared in the doorway, a bag of eggs in her hand, and took a step in. Dad yanked her arm and jammed it behind her back. She dropped the eggs. He locked his free arm around her throat. He must have loosened his hold because she let out a scream that seemed almost not human.

I sprang off the floor, unsure of what to do. He folded her arm more. The room was tense. The air was electric. Then, I heard another sound. The snapping of a bone. The crack echoed across the room. Dad seemed not to have heard, or it appeared he didn't. Mom collapsed; her arm bent oddly out of place. He crouched down to her level, his eyes raking over her busted arm. In a voice that was coarse and earthy, he whispered, *"You're late."*

Getting a job had been Mom's idea.

Shortly after we moved to El Dorado, Mom told Dad there was more money going out than coming in. She had to get a job. Initially, he said nothing. Dad didn't want Mom to work. He believed the man should support the family, and the woman should stay home and take care of the house, cook the meals. The main reason, though, was he wanted her away from other people.

Eyes focused, he scanned each bill and carefully examined the check registry. When he was done, he slumped in the chair. Dad sat quietly. His eyes grew dark. He reminded Mom that she belonged to him. She bobbed her head in agreement. His face sank as he gazed at the pile of bills. He lifted his fists and slammed them on the table. "You better stay away from other men!" he shouted.

Mom agreed. "Yes, Frankie," but rolled her eyes when she walked away.

She had the McDonald's job within a week. Before I left for school one morning, Mom dropped a key in my hand. I was to wear it around my neck, on a string, and let myself in after school. I never forgot to wear it. It was the only piece of jewelry I owned.

Dad had his own worries. One day, when Mom was in another room, he whispered to me that I had to keep track of what time she got back from work in the afternoons. I nodded, but I never looked at the clock. I told Dad the same time every day.

When I look back now at my father, through a lens not crafted by him, I no longer see a grainy image of a man who is king of his castle, but one with ominous clarity of a young zealot who, using the same mallet he used to build his kingdom, obliterated it into a million pieces.

In retrospect, this period of my life was carving away the bond between my mother and me, like a dune slammed by wave after wave. There were strained moments when Dad told me to do more than listen at the bathroom door. He told me to trail her in the bathroom, watching, when he wasn't home. I never did. She slammed the door in my face when I first tried to follow her in.

Mom didn't like me spying on her any more than I wanted to do it. Every time Dad ordered me to chronicle my mother's actions, parts of our mother–daughter relationship were washed away, scattered into heaps, then dragged away grain by grain.

CHAPTER 2:

TWILIGHT ZONE

—

The story of how trash bags came to be fastened across our entire home is a bizarre one. Something inside my dad shifted a few years earlier when his grandmother, Cora, died. It was as though he kept himself in line for her. Cora lived with Dad's rich aunt and uncle in their monstrous home. There was a working water fountain in the long hallway, a pool in the backyard, and a sunken den with a pool table, slot machines, and a giant marlin on the wall. Dad's aunt Patsy had a son my age. I loved going there. It was a magical place, and my cousins got to live there every single day.

Immediately after Cora died, Dad became estranged from his family and yanked us away into total isolation. I never saw any of my aunts, uncles, or cousins on his side of the family again. During holidays, Dad would go off on his own and visit them. Once, Mom confronted him about why he didn't take his family with him, and he told her he was ashamed of us.

When we moved from Louisiana to Arkansas, a dark lens slid over him. He saw men everywhere, his eyes constantly darting. As long as I can remember, he talked about men, but after we moved, it was as though his mind was dragged into the Twilight Zone. He'd reached a dimension of reality that only he could see. When I looked around my town, my little sliced section of the world, I saw trees with low hanging limbs. Flowers pushing up out the ground. Families walking. Looking at the same scene, my father saw villains, men who were as numberless as stars, all coming to rip his wife away from him.

The trash bag episode happened one Saturday when Mom, Bubba, and I came back from grocery shopping. Dad had been anxiously pacing the house. We had taken too long. Mom tried to explain that the store had been packed, and the lines were long. But Dad would hear none of it. He grabbed me by the shoulders and demanded to know who she had been with. Had we seen any men? I explained to him we had not spoken to anyone. He accused me of lying and squeezed my shoulders so tightly I thought his fingers would snip my arms off.

Dad fetched a hammer and nails and began pounding the window frames shut. Once all the windows were secured, we spent the remainder of the day unrolling trash bags and tacking them straight and taut across windows. After the first layer was done, Dad's eyes raked over our handiwork. His face reddened, and his skin turned clammy. He took a long pause, then said the men could still see through the bags. We started unrolling more trash bags.

Dad handed me a few dollars to fetch some more tacks. I charged down the road to the store as fast as I could, afraid the sun would set before we could completely block out the men. It couldn't wait another day. A real desperation grew inside of me. I didn't understand why the men were after my mom. The bags gave us the advantage of cover, I reasoned.

When we were finished, Dad tacked drapes over the trash bags and told us we weren't allowed to remove any of the tacks or peek out of the windows. That night, he dragged Bubba's sleeping bag out the closet and told him he'd start sleeping against the front door whenever Dad had to work nights. The men, he told us, would try to get in. Bubba's job was to block the door with his body. I studied my brother's anxious face. He looked brave.

———

THE EARTH WAS SHAKING. My eyes ripped open. I held my breath as otherworldly screams tunneled through the walls and bore their way through the several layers of quilts I was hiding under. Within seconds, Mom bolted out of bed. I threw the covers aside and scrambled behind. Dad said I couldn't be more than two feet away from Mom when he worked the graveyard shift. We raced toward the screams.

The night before, Dad had locked the back door with the only skeleton key and taken it with him because he had to work. Bubba was stuffed in his sleeping bag wedged against the front door while Dad was gone. I often wondered why men were outside our home, and if they were so bad, why Dad didn't call the police. He told me to sleep in the same bed as Mom. If she got up for any reason, I had to follow.

That morning, Dad had come home from work and unlocked the front door, but instead of it knocking against Bubba, it swung wide open. Bubba had rolled a few feet away from it in his sleep. Dad, enraged and still wearing his steel-toed boots, began shouting and kicking Bubba all over the house as he was still trapped in the sleeping bag. Bubba pled and cried for him to stop.

After a few moments, Dad finally gave up the kicking and yelling, and stormed into the kitchen. He tried to slam the chef's door behind him, but it just swung rapidly back and forth, stiffly losing the momentum that had been thrust upon its hinges.

I looked over to see Bubba crumpled up in the sleeping bag. He looked oddly like a giant brown caterpillar trying to scoot across the ground. Only he wasn't scooting, just moaning. For a moment, I thought he was dead. Mom walked over and helped him out his sleeping bag. He stood up as though he were an old man, worn, fragile, his eyes bulging as they raked across the room, trying to make sense of what just happened. He huffed, then walked slumped over as though he were struggling to carry a bundle of bricks in his arms. When he crawled under the covers, he deflated and closed his eyes, unmoving.

Mom sat on the edge of the bed and folded her arms across her swollen belly. I stared at curvy silhouettes of toys while Dad's voice boomed in the background about how many men probably got past Bubba during the night. I imagined the men, single file, marching through the door at night, stepping over my sleeping brother, yanking my mother from her bed. I pictured her being dragged down the road, screaming for her life. Then Dad shouted something that threw me off: SHE COULD HAVE GOTTEN OUT!

Did he mean Mom? Did he mean she could have escaped? Why would she escape?

I thought about the sleeping bag Dad had bought me a few months prior that sat in the corner of my closet unused, and I began to worry if I would be the next person sleeping on the cold floor. Moments later, he rushed in the room. I mashed my eyes shut. Mom howled as she was dragged away.

Forty years later, my brother's screams would still echo in my head. I'd hear them every time a sleeping bag unzipped, or the chill of a wood floor rushed through my bare feet. It wasn't a moment in time I wanted to remember, but Aunt Carol never taught me how to erase memories. She never told me how to leave them behind.

Chapter 3:

Promised Land

—

Gabby arrived in late fall. Ms. Buckley, the school principal, entered my classroom and fixed her gaze on me. "It's a girl!" she shouted and tossed her hands in the air as though, together, we had all won an Olympic event. Everyone cheered. One boy jumped up from his desk and started high fiving everyone around him. It was a fantastic moment. Once my baby sister was in my arms, I ran my finger down the curve of her nose and whispered in her ear that I would always protect her. I remember searching her face and arms, looking for some type of flaw, counting her wiggling fingers and toes over and over again. She was perfect.

A few Sundays later, I biked home from the railroad to get ready for church. After I had wiped the day's grime from my face and neck and thrown some church clothes on, Mom ushered us into the car, smoothing my puffy hair as we walked. "Your hair needs brushing," she said.

"It is brushed," I replied.

Mom grimaced and stepped into the car.

When we arrived at church, I looked for my cousins and convinced them to sit with us. Their parents were musicians and usually played instruments or sang at the beginning and end of service. My uncle Joe strummed his guitar, while Aunt Sue stepped to the front of the pulpit to sing a solo. Tall stained-glass windows reflected a prism of light behind her as her voice rang through the church.

As we were standing, waiting for the song to end, Josephine nudged me. I turned to see her stick her tongue out at Jack, who stood on the other side of Bubba. He tried to reach across Bubba and take a swipe at her.

When the music was done, we took our seats, as my uncle and aunt slipped into a pew in the front. The evangelist grabbed a Bible from a pew and made his way to the pulpit. Jack, sucking his cheeks, glared at Josephine, who had been giving him a hard time all day.

The evangelist was short-statured like my dad, but he wore a nice suit that made one almost not notice his height. The first thing he said in a booming voice was that God was in the house. Everyone clapped. I glanced over at Jack and Josephine, still taking swipes at each other across my brother. I scanned the crowd for any signs of God or angels watching my cousins. I didn't want to be involved in some type of church brawl. My cousins were making me nervous. I scooted further down.

"I am going to talk tonight about faith," the evangelist declared, hoisting the Bible into the air. The congregation was hushed as he continued, "I'm going start with Abraham and the Promised Land."

I cocked an eyebrow at that remark. *Did he just say, "Promised Land?"* I slid to the edge of the pew to hear better.

He talked about how Abraham walked in faith, not knowing where he was going, though, obviously he had a good pair of shoes to go the distance. The evangelist started doing jazz hands and walking fast in place behind the pulpit shouting, "Walk it off! Walk it off!" as the congregation roared in laughter. Abraham didn't just put his faith in God; he also put faith in himself and in his soul. I looked down at my shoes and decided that I was going to try it myself. I was going to pull an Abraham.

I SPENT DAYS FEVERISHLY thinking about how-to walk-in faith, when one morning, on my way to school, I stepped on a nail. It wasn't a long nail, just long enough to prick my foot and let me know it was there. As I sat down on the sidewalk to wedge it out, a thought occurred to me: *If I can feel something as I walk, maybe that will remind me to walk in faith.* I grabbed a notebook and tore out half a page. With my pencil, I scratched out a few words to form a sentence, the one thing that I wanted the most.

I want a family that cares about me.

I folded it neatly into a little square, then covered it with the inner sole of my shoe. My sole had something in it now for me to believe in. I wasn't sure if it was the same as walking in faith, but it gave me hope that one day, God might chuck a new family my way.

I ran to school, jumping over the broken pieces of sidewalk and landing solidly on my feet. The little wad of paper pressed against my skin, reminding me it was there. I wasn't just walking in faith; I was running, jumping, and leaping in it. Life would get better. I willed myself to believe that I could find happiness, that the words in my sole were going to lead me there.

Each day, as I walked mile after mile, every inch of ground became important to me. The beautiful oak trees that lined the streets became old, affectionate friends. Their long oak arms extended to me, high fiving me on my daily walks, their leafy branches passing through my hair. The cracks in the sidewalks no longer grimaced at me, but smiled brightly, waiting for my reciprocation. Tiny purple wisteria petals carpeted my walk, kicking up into the air as I stirred them with my feet. The world, every rock and cranny, even the white clouds that floated above, involved me. I was slowly becoming part of this lucid, beautiful world.

Over the course of a few weeks, I continued adding slips of papers into my sneakers.

I don't want to struggle anymore.
I want to be liked.
I want good things to happen.

It felt as though I finally had some say in who I was. I had made up my mind. I was taking my life back.

―――

A KNOT WAS PULSING on the back of my head, like my brain was trying to push its way out. Bulging, swelling, screaming at me. *Where am I?* I must have passed out for a few moments. It was evening, past suppertime; my eyes settled on blurry and distorted images, as though I were peering through Aunt Carol's trifocals. A baby was wailing. *Gabby.* I tried to raise myself up but felt dizzy. One of the images rushed at me, yanked me to my feet. A lightning bolt flashed through my brain as Dad gripped my throat. I remembered the evening in shreds.

A few days earlier, Dad bought a Raleigh Grand Prix with chrome wheels and gumwall tires from someone. He told us that he was keeping the bike in the den because he didn't want anyone stealing it out of the garage.

The evening of the knot, Bubba and I were in the den playing. He had received a train set for Christmas—a twin-engine diesel with freight cars, flat cars, boxcars, and a matching Chessie caboose with a real operating whistle and crossing gate. We put our hands on the plywood and felt the vibrations as it barreled, full blast, around the little track.

The chef's door that separated the kitchen from the dining room swung open. Dad shuffled in, lugging Gabby. He told me to keep an eye on her and not to allow her near the bike. She was six months old now, crawling. I sighed once he was gone. It wasn't often Bubba let me play with his trains, and now I had to babysit. I plopped on the floor to play with Gabby. I kept peering back at Bubba as he struggled to put some track pieces back together that kept popping loose each time the train circled, derailing all the cars.

"Do you need some help?" I finally asked.

"I can't get it to snap together."

I left Gabby playing with a rattle, which she didn't seem to be too interested in. Pushing Bubba aside, I took over the train track repair. About a minute passed, then there was a loud *thud*, followed by a wail. I spun around to see blood oozing from a half-inch slice on her forehead. She had crawled to the Raleigh bike and tried to pull herself up, but she slipped, and her tiny head came down on the pointy edge of a pedal. Bubba grabbed her while I raced for help.

Before I made it to the chef's door, it flew open. "What's going on?" Dad roared.

My mother sprang to Gabby, whose face was stained with blood. I stood frozen, ready to cry. Bubba's eyes were wide as he stared at me. One of us was going to take the hit for this.

"Gabby fell on the bike and gashed her head," I whimpered.

"I told you to watch her!"

I braced as Dad's fist swung toward me. With all his might, he struck my left cheekbone. I flew sideways several feet and landed solidly on the floor, the back of my head hitting a corner of a half wall. I lay on my side on the floor, unable to move, a black vortex swirling above me.

I managed to make out the image of my father rushing toward me, but I had no time to react. Dad yanked me from the floor onto my feet, then gripped my throat with his hands. The vortex returned, but only for seconds. He shouted that Bubba and I had to go with my mom to the hospital so that Gabby could get stitches. I couldn't open my left eye at all. Dad said something about me guarding my mom as she talked to the doctors. I heard parts of, "Don't let her go anywhere with the doctors by herself.

Keep an eye on her at all times." He told me I was in charge of that—*if I can be trusted to do anything right*. I was pretty sure I could keep an eye on her, though at the time, I only had sight in one of them.

———

"WE SHOULD HAVE BROUGHT the trains," Bubba said.

He and I were patiently sitting in a waiting area, while my mom and Gabby went into a room with the doctor. We both knew that we would get punished if Dad found out that our mother was unsupervised, but the doctor didn't want too many people around while he stitched up Gabby's forehead.

"The trains are the reason we're here," I said as I rubbed the goose egg that was swelling on the back of my head.

"Oh." He looked down at his hands. "Why do we always have to watch Gabby?"

"Somebody has to do it."

Bubba sighed. "A puppy would have been so much easier."

After she received stitches, Bubba and I were allowed to see Gabby. I hoped that my mother wouldn't tell my father that she was alone with the doctor, since both of us would get hit.

A steely-haired nurse did a double-take when she noticed my swelling eye. She asked what had happened. I glanced at my mother and knew I was to protect my father. I lied and said that I fell.

She looked at me suspiciously. "Both you and your sister fell? At the same time?"

"Yes, ma'am."

I watched as she looked from Gabby, to me, then back to Gabby again. At first, I thought she wasn't going to believe it. I could feel a bead of sweat running down the nape of my neck. I checked to make sure it wasn't blood. No one knew about the knot on the back of my head, which had now doubled in size. My head thrummed with a dull ache, and I wanted desperately to sit back down. What was the probability that both Gabby and I had fallen at the same time? I didn't know. The nurse must have known, because she looked at me for a long moment, before leaning down to continue to write on a clipboard about Gabby. With her gaze on the paper, she mentioned to me, "You need to put an ice pack on your eye to keep it from swelling." Then she walked out of the room, and I didn't see her again.

On the ride home, my head pounded. I thought of the nurse. Had she really believed that story? I was only eight years old, and I wouldn't have believed it. It was then that I understood most adults couldn't be trusted. Certainly, somehow, the nurse could have helped us. But it would have been too much trouble, too much paperwork, a whole other clipboard.

Later that evening, it was just a series of frames recorded in my memory as a moving picture—of Bubba quietly playing in a corner with a single train, of Mom swaddling Gabby in a wooden rocker, and of Dad hovering over Mom, shouting, because he found out that the doctor was a man.

CHAPTER 4:

WIND HORSE

It was during a fourth-grade field trip that I made my first friend. We shared a seat as the bus bumped down the road to the zoo. She wasn't in my class, but I had seen her on the playground during recess. On the bus she mentioned that she forgot her lunch box at school. I told her we could split what I had in mine—a ham sandwich that Mom had quartered, a sandwich bag stuffed full of chips, two cookies, and a thermos full of Tang.

"My name is Sarah," she said. I shyly smiled, as though I had never met another human before. After I told her my name was Tracie, she hesitated, as in deep thought, then replied, "Are you Trash Bag Tracie?" I shifted away from her and gazed out the window. Within seconds, I felt a hand press on my arm. I snapped my head back, expecting her to laugh at me. "I think that's a cool nickname," she said. "Somebody told me you're the smartest kid in school."

I NEEDED A PLACE, besides the empty schoolyard and oil refinery, to get away from Dad and his weekend rages. There was one problem; I had nowhere to go. So, when Sarah mentioned that I could go to her house Sunday after church, I was thrilled. She drew a map on a sheet of notebook paper and handed it to me. That Sunday after church, I shoveled my plate of food into my mouth as fast as I could before I charged outside. I pedaled a few miles down cracked sidewalks and asphalt roads, until I reached the house number jotted on the paper. Sarah's house was tall and stunning, with soaring windows you could see right into and blue irises that lined a walkway. I reached to knock on the door, but it swung open before I could.

"I can't believe you came," Sarah said, then marched me through her home like I was royalty. Inside was a ceiling that shot up about thirty feet and a staircase with a huge grand piano beside it. She introduced me to both her parents before we settled onto a tufted sofa the color of an avocado. The windows shone brightly, reflecting light off the sparkling floors. We laughed and giggled about different kids at school. She gushed about her horse that stayed at their family ranch, just outside of town. When a car drove past and its engine backfired, we both turned toward the window, startled, then began a fit of giggling. When we stopped, I glanced out to see if the car was still there.

"You get to look out windows?" I said.

"Of course," she said. "Can't you?"

I shrugged, like I didn't understand the question.

Moments later, both her parents appeared, her mom offering glasses of iced tea. She was a tall, slender woman in her mid-thirties, with a warm voice and olive skin that glowed from the light shining in. I took a glass and thanked her, quietly sipping it, as Sarah's father asked me if I liked horses. I said yes. He must have liked my answer because in response he grinned widely. He ambled to a corner of the room. I studied him as he thumbed through some vinyl records. He had an angular face and slender build and walked with a slight swagger, as if at any second, he would break out into a dance.

He slipped a disc into a console. A man's voice crooned from the wooden box. Moments later, the room reverberated powerfully with an ensemble of wind instruments and a mixture of horns. The music had my body numbed from head to toe, breathless. Every note clanged powerfully through the room. Her dad tapped his feet and snapped his thumbs, his fleshy clicks adding another dimension to the lyrical melody that had me captivated. I'd never heard anything with so many harmonious elements. Sarah's mother hollered over the instrumentals, asking me if I liked Big Band music. Still breathless from the sounds that had taken control of the room, I merely nodded. Sarah jerked to her feet and grabbed her mother's hand. They danced in the center of the room as the sun poured in through the window, making it look like they were shimmering gold.

They must have thought I was absurd when I stood up and drifted to the bright window so that I could stare outside and press my hand on the cool glass. I peered with a fresh pair of eyes, not the eyes of a child, but the eyes of someone who was testing the boundaries of freedom. I cocked my head with this twisted concept that maybe this could be my new reality. I imagined one day I, too, could look through panes of glass at the world, free and clear, without Dad blacking out my view of it. Then I wondered something I had never thought of before: *Was Dad trying to keep people from seeing in, or keep us from seeing out?*

During the week at school, Sarah invited me to go to their ranch outside of town. She said they normally went on Saturdays. I told her I'd ask my parents, but I didn't. Saturday morning, I biked to their home and told them Mom and Dad said I could go. Her parents raised their eyebrows in question but said nothing. We all loaded into their green-and-brown station wagon, and after a few minutes, Sarah's dad pulled into a little crimson donut shop. A metal donut sat on top of a white neon sign that blinked Spudnuts. Sarah told me the donuts—made from potato flour—were the best donuts in town. Her father brought back a boxful, and soon, we were banging down the road to the ranch.

The drive took less than a half hour. As we neared the estate, edges of the road were chromatic with flowers, which seemed ablaze, in contrast to the green pastures that rolled behind them.

We pulled up to a grand horseshoe-shaped gate with a big *B* on it. Her father got out of the station wagon to open it. As we rolled under the wrought-iron horseshoe, I cracked my window a bit to stare up at the entry, into the world of wealth. There were scenic ridges and hills all around us. The air tasted like vanilla and lavender.

The house was a two-story terra-cotta colonial with massive white columns. Wild daisies traveled from the gate, all the way up to the front door, welcoming us eagerly. The grounds were just as elaborate as the home itself, with an in-ground pool and colonial pool house that could double as a guest home. For the horses, there were multiple barns and fenced-in paddocks. A riding arena, round pen, and an event course were near the barns. There were also dozens of riding trails that traversed the property.

At the barn, Sarah handed me the reins to a small pony named Goldie. With my free hand, I reached out and stroked Goldie's long face and neck.

An hour later, I was galloping down a winding trail with Sarah and her parents. When my pony rounded a corner too fast, I was chucked into a pile of pine needles, and I immediately sprang to my feet, searching for cover. I did *not* want to get back on, but Sarah's dad explained to me that the pony was old and gentle. I needed to face my fear and get back on. I stood motionless, barely breathing. I don't remember what he said to me next, but I do remember this: my fear suddenly turned to bravery. A minute later, I gripped the reins in my hand as he hoisted me back in the saddle. By the time we rounded the bend, I knew I'd made the right decision.

My breath caught at the sight of a crystal lake, sparkling like a thousand diamonds. It was then that I knew I had to come back to this place. I relished in the idea that I belonged here, convincing myself that if I never told my parents about it, then it wasn't a lie.

———

EVERY SATURDAY, I HOPPED on my bike and pedaled to their house, and before they could ask if my parents gave me permission, I'd say, "My parents are *so* grateful you are letting me go to the ranch." Minutes later, we were bumping down the road, singing along to big band music on the radio and stuffing our mouths with Spudnuts.

Sarah's dad, whom I now called Poppy, handed me the reins to a chestnut mare one day and said that I was ready for lessons. He hoisted me up into the saddle and patiently taught me how to keep my reins short and stay balanced in the saddle. Poppy said the one thing I needed to remember was to pat my horse every chance I got.

By the time fall ended, I knew how to properly mount a horse and to keep my body straight and upright. I no longer fell off or kept a death grip on the reins. By the end of spring, I was riding like a pro.

One Saturday, Sarah's mom told me to invite my parents to the ranch.

"It will be fun," she said. "I'm sure your parents would enjoy themselves."

There was a part of me that wanted to give the invitation to my parents. I imagined myself proudly explaining to them that I knew rich people who wanted them to visit their ranch. I'd explain about the horses and fancy landscaping and the private lakes that could be fished on. But when I pictured my parents visiting the ranch with my friend's family, an alarm clanged inside my head, signaling my return to reality. *What if Dad talked about the men? What if Sarah's dad was one of them?* My father would never mesh with their world, so I kept them camouflaged in the background of mine. I imagined Dad, yanking a clump of hair at my scalp, and dragging me away from a world that contained men who were not him.

Poppy would often tell us the legend of Wind Horse, a beast seasoned by no man. Sarah and I would sit big-eyed and breathless each time he told it, and we never tired of hearing it. There were millions of horses across the world, but none like Wind Horse, wild like a bolt of lightning, yet gentle like the wind.

Wind Horse was fearless. When needed, he would appear like a rush of water, engulf the person who needed his help with love, and carry that person to safety. But he thrived on being free and belonging to no one.

According to Poppy, one day Wind Horse heard a child crying and went to offer his aid. He found it was a small Indian boy whose foot had been cut off by a bear trap. Wind Horse knelt to let the boy crawl onto his back. He realized that the boy could not live with such a bad wound, so he decided to bring him to the Great Hunting Ground, a place of no return.

Wind Horse knew the boy couldn't travel by himself, so he walked the path with the boy, knowing there would be no coming back. As they traveled, the two began to bond as one. Wind Horse knew that the farther he walked, the less freedom he had. The path started to change drastically, and Wind Horse started to feel the fear of the boy. Wind Horse gave his life to carry the boy forward, and together they fulfilled their last journey. Poppy said that every time a strong breeze blew by, we should remember that Wind Horse was watching over us too.

"But he is with the boy!" I shouted.

"Wind Horse is wherever the wind blows," he answered.

It was a sad and happy story at the same time, but always at the end, Poppy would jump up and grab each of us under an arm and act like he was galloping with us. Then he would lightly toss us on a sofa, before pretending to die on the hard tile or a recliner. In fits of laughter, we would always shout, "Tell us again!"

He had lots of stories about horses, but the story of Wind Horse was my favorite. Sometimes at night, if my dad was in the next room, screaming at my mom or beating her, I told the story over and over to myself, in soft whispers, until I eventually fell asleep.

Chapter 5:

Video Game

—

"I've got some exciting news," Mom announced. "We're moving back to Louisiana."

We had lived in El Dorado for nearly three years—longer than any place we'd lived before.

"Why?" I asked. All I could think about was Sarah, her parents, and the horses.

"Your dad took a better job. It'll be great. Like a fresh start."

My cousins, Jack and Josephine, had moved back to Louisiana a few months earlier, and Dad was going to work at the same refinery that Uncle Bob did.

Mom continued about how we could meet bona fide Cajun people, and she could learn to make Cajun food. Her eyes sparkled when she talked about finding our own place in the country. We could live the high life, like genuine frontier people in the *Little House on the Prairie* books, only with alligators and swamps, instead of bison and prairies.

I wasn't as excited as Mom was. After everything I had been through, I was going to have to start all over. Dad sold his boat, and we spent almost the entire day tightly packing our furniture and boxes into a U-Haul. Sarah's family was out of town, so I had no way to tell her that we were moving.

Early the next morning, the moving truck roared out of the driveway, with Dad behind the wheel. The rest of us followed in the car, with Mom driving. We rolled past the sidewalks Bubba and I had ridden on over and over again and past the school, with a hole in the fence that we often crawled through. Then the car went up and over the railroad tracks I'd walked on so many times. I took one last look behind me at El Dorado fading into the distance, before turning back to stare at the taillights of the U-Haul in front of us that started picking up speed. I held on as Mom pressed hard on the gas pedal and shouted, "Louisiana, here we come!"

OUR NEXT HOME WAS half of a duplex located in a town that had a giant lake called False River, which was almost eleven miles-long. During the summer months, locals and tourists floated along the bank, casting fishing lines from their boats and dipping their feet into the cool water. My cousins lived in a mobile home park along the water's edge. Sometimes Jack would take Bubba and me fishing—we caught an eel once—and we'd walk back to his home with fish for his mom to fry. Josephine was starting to like boys and spent a lot of time on the phone.

There was a fenced pasture near the entrance of the mobile park with a single horse. I often found myself gravitating toward the fence, with an apple or a clump of sweet-smelling grass. It made me homesick for Sarah. I became obsessed with collecting horse magazines, small horse statues, and anything and everything else having to do with horses. I had miniature horses, iron ones with tiny chain harnesses that Grandma Avis found at a garage sale. I kept them sitting on the edge of my dresser or in my hand as I slept. Posters of different types of horses lined my walls. And my horse addiction only grew with time; it represented to me the life I secretly held. I wanted those moments back. The laughter, the sunshine, the love. Purple flower petals, ducks, Spudnuts. All of it was gone.

A few months later, Mom once again announced that we were moving, only this time to a place with fewer people living around us.

"I guess Dad doesn't like having so many neighbors," Bubba said to me.

"Or men," I replied.

THE MEMORY OF SARAH continued to stay with me. It was as if the last year had been scripted and rehearsed, like a stage play. In my memory, I pictured each day with them as a scene. I remembered all the words, all the lines. Every moment led to the final act, which was my departure. The performances were Oscar-worthy, the ending heartbreaking.

I yearned to be back on the ranch, so badly. I made a promise to myself to be rich and successful one day and have a ranch of my own. I scribbled that idea on another slip of paper and stuffed it in my shoe. *I want to be somebody important.* It was a desire that was carefully carved inside of me, and somewhere in that part of me, someone had dropped a ball of fire that burned deep and pure, guiding me to wherever it was I supposed to be.

When we moved again, it was to a large white farmhouse with a tin roof out in the middle of nowhere, just like my parents wanted. Secluded. A lonely Chinese woman took to visiting my mother several times a week. Dad resented Mom having a friend. "Make her go away," he said. "Or I will." He felt that Mom was too slow in ending the friendship with the woman, so he flung the furniture around and beat Mom every day, until she made the Chinese woman go away. My mother told me after the fact that she'd left a note clipped on the front screen door for the lady, explaining that they couldn't be friends anymore, and that the woman had knocked until she finally gave up and left bawling.

"Why did we move from El Dorado?" I asked. "Things were better there. We didn't have to make Chinese people cry."

"Well, she got on my nerves, anyway," Mom said. "Frontier people don't fraternize with the Chinese. There are too many cultural differences."

"We had a good life before," I said.

"This is our life now. You need to appreciate it," she replied.

Back in El Dorado, I had lived above the struggles of being poor, at least on the weekends. I had glimpsed the lifestyle of the rich, temporarily set free, unshackled, and unencumbered. It had given me a taste of freedom. I was keenly aware that money, or the lack of it, could either imprison a person or liberate them.

I decided that one day it would liberate me.

GABBY GOT IN THE habit of breaking my things. While I was at school, she opened my dresser drawers to use as a makeshift ladder and climbed to the top to reach whatever was sitting up there. On a Friday afternoon, I was looking for my gumball machine that was a Christmas gift from Aunt Sue. I found it under my bed, shattered, with most of the gumballs missing and a hammer lying next to it.

"Mom!" I screamed while running into the kitchen with the deceased gumball machine in hand.

"What is it? You sound like the house is on fire."

"Worse than that," I cried. "Look what Gabby did!"

"Well, what have I told you about keeping your things out of her reach? It's your own fault."

"It was on top of my dresser and my door was closed."

"You should have put it higher."

"The only place higher is the ceiling."

"Look, I don't have time to hear about your trivial problems because you aren't responsible with your things. It's just a stupid gumball machine. It was a clearance item worth ten cents."

"I'm going to take care of this myself," I said as I tried to reach for Gabby.

Mom grabbed my hand as Gabby peeked from behind her, wide-eyed and grinning. "Don't you dare lay a hand on her. You have to go through me first."

I yanked my hand away as Gabby, from the safety of Mom's shadow, stuck her tongue out at me. She was my mother's Laura Ingalls Wilder, and Bubba and I were the free-range chickens roaming the yard. It was starting to take its toll on both of us.

When Dad got home from work that evening, I waited until he settled in his recliner in front of the television before I approached him about the gumball machine. I felt like Gabby should have been punished for it. I also wanted it replaced. I waited for him to look at me, but he didn't. I cleared my throat and spoke, nervously recounting the story about how she had gone in my room and taken it off my dresser while I was at school, how she'd smashed it with a hammer. Dad never looked away from the television. He took a long sip of a beer he was holding in his hand and acted as though I weren't there at all. I nervously shifted from one foot to the other, studying the creamy edges of the window frame beside him. After a few moments, his gaze still on the flickering of the screen, he asked me why I wasn't more responsible with my stuff.

The same mind that had dragged me to Dad to complain had nothing to say. I stood completely still, brainless. He waited a few seconds for me to speak then started a lecture about how I should keep things out of Gabby's reach and needed to learn how to take care of my things. At the end of his speech, he told me to do twenty-five laps around the house and, also, a ten-page essay on being responsible. I lurched out the door, fists clenched.

I remembered the evening in layers. The more I thought about how

Gabby hadn't been reprimanded, not even sharp words, the angrier I got. I ran faster. When I reached my twenty-fifth lap, I continued running around the house until I was breathless and couldn't go anymore. I collapsed on the back porch, half wondering about the whole event.

My parents had sent me a message through the crushed gumball machine: I would always be the equivalent of an employee, my mother's sentry, a watchkeeper. There were more responsibilities in my childhood than memories of being a child.

I didn't do the essay.

The next week, Dad lectured Bubba and me about why we were to be dentists, seemingly unaware that neither of us cared to be sticking our fingers in the mouths of complete strangers. A half hour later, he announced that we were ready to do a one-hundred-page essay on dentistry, due in seven days, and we were to memorize the Preamble to the Constitution. He also announced that we were to add a hundred sit-ups, jumping jacks, and push-ups to our daily routine. Bubba began to slump further and further on the sofa, utterly worn out by the intensity of the subject, his eyelids drooping more and more as Dad droned on about dentistry and exercise. Bubba seemed to care less than I did, but to be fair, he was only ten years old.

That weekend, our parents went into town and left Gabby with us. She was sitting in the living room watching television as I worked on homework and my dentist essay. I put down my notebook and pencil to get a textbook out of my room. When I got back, she had scribbled all over my homework and was stabbing Dad's new leather recliner with the pencil. I grabbed it from her and called Bubba in to ask him what we should do.

"This would be a good time to memorize the Declaration of Independence," he said.

"I don't think the Declaration of Independence is going to save us," I replied.

We both looked at Gabby, who was now bent down on the floor, trying desperately to stand on her head. She toppled over with a thud.

That evening, Bubba and I met our parents at the door and tried to explain what had happened, but it only enraged Dad. He rushed at my brother and with one swoop of his arm picked up Bubba as though he were as light as a cotton ball and crushed him into the wall.

We were good for nothing, Dad shouted. He dropped his hands but

Bubba, winded and looking petrified, was stuck in the drywall, which was now cracked with the imprint of a ten-year-old body.

"Look what you've done to the wall!" Dad hollered at Bubba. He grabbed me by the throat and flung me onto the sofa. "We can't have anything nice because of you two."

"Daddy, look, I can stand on my head," Gabby exclaimed. We all looked over at Gabby and started clapping, except for Bubba, who was quietly sobbing that he *could* say a few lines of the Declaration of Independence.

If I could have frozen the moment in time, the cracked drywall in our home narrated the story of our lives. There were some holes pocked in the walls the size of a fist, chronicling a drunken burst of anger here and there, but then there was the one in our living room that told a more powerful story. This hole was about a foot wide and two feet long. It wasn't a fist that made the wall explode. It was my brother's back.

IT WAS A HUMID SUMMER. Clouds hung in the sky, dragged from the Gulf of Mexico, bringing with them warm and spongy air, so steamy that when I rode my bike, my shirt would be soaked within minutes.

Dad decided it was time to move again. Once more we packed all our things and moved to another town. I had just finished the sixth grade. Behind our new home, facing a different street, was a clapboard house with an older couple living in it. Their fourteen-year-old granddaughter lived with them. Her name was Lena. Mom got a job at a pharmacy and had to work weekends.

One Saturday someone knocked on the back door. It was Lena. She asked if I wanted to play a video game. I said I would and led her to the living room where my Atari console sat, cradled on a stand. She had never come over before. We played in silence. I sat close to the TV; she sat behind me. When the game was finished, I looked back to ask if she wanted to play again. My hand hovered over the controller. I didn't know what to say. Lena was perched on my dad's lap, running her fingers through his hair. His hands were massaging her sides, his eyes were closed, and he was kissing her neck.

It had never registered with me why my dad beat my mother—the true meaning of it. But I was reaching, or had reached, an age of understanding things. As I aged and began wrestling myself for answers between what was right and wrong, I became more cognizant of the good and bad doings of my dad, as though I peered at him through a polarized lens. I no longer saw him through the innocent eyes of a child. His wicked actions saturated a darkness in my mind. I'd never seen him kiss my mother like this, but I had seen his fingers curled around her neck, choking the life out of her. Staring at him, gently kissing someone else, I understood. I understood the scale of how wrong the beatings were and how more wrong him holding someone who wasn't my mother was. My mind was utter blackness as I scrutinized them.

His eyes popped open to see me watching, so he told her they would take it elsewhere. She nodded as they stood up together. Dad told me to watch the back door and if anyone drove up, I was to holler. Then, fingers intertwined, they walked into my parent's room and shut the door.

That summer, Lena came over whenever Mom went to work, according to my memory. After the first time, she didn't bother knocking anymore. Mom would pull out the driveway and then, as if on cue, Lena would appear in the doorway. Dad would lead her into his bedroom. Time and time again, Dad hollered for me to watch for a car driving up. She never again asked to play the game. I'd wait awkwardly by myself. After about twenty minutes, the bedroom door would open and, without making eye contact with me, Lena would slip outside.

When Lena turned fifteen, Mom told me to pick her out a birthday gift. I felt conflicted about it and told her I didn't know what to get, so maybe we could just skip the gift. "Tracie," she said, "you should learn to be kind to those less fortunate than you. Lena doesn't have any parents. You do."

I picked out an Air Supply tape and a tape case. Mom bought some wrapping paper and a bow, and after we got home, I watched her singing and grinning as she wrapped it. She felt good about doing something nice for someone. Mom had a good heart for others, and even if Dad hadn't threatened me, I probably wouldn't have told Mom anything I knew. I brought the gift to Lena. She made a face when she saw what it was and asked if Mom was working the next morning. I said she was. After Lena slipped in and out the next morning, I didn't feel right anymore about her coming over when Mom was at work.

Mom worked as a cashier at a drugstore called Eckerds. She wafted through the back door one day nearly in tears and told me she thought she might get fired. I asked her what happened. She was shaking so much she had to lay down as she told the story—how Dad was always in and out of the store on days she worked, following her around, chatting. That day, an elderly couple had stopped her to ask her where the cough syrup was. Dad was still chatting at her. Mom told him to hang on while she helped the customers. He shouted at the top of his lungs, his booming voice echoing through the cavernous building, that *he came first*. The elderly couple didn't wait for an answer but just skittered away, coughing. "It was so embarrassing," she said, her voice quivering. I could see her chest rising as she took deep breaths to calm her nerves. "This is why I can't keep a job," she whispered. "He watches me at work." Mom closed her eyes and lay silent. I often wondered where Dad went on the weekends. Now I knew. When Lena wasn't around, he would often leave. My job was to babysit Gabby, so I rarely left home. I bit my bottom lip as I watched Mom's chest heave up and down. Lena had been over earlier in the day. Dad had left right after she did. He must have gone to Eckerds.

The next day, I asked Dad if he was dating Lena. Normally, I wouldn't have asked a question so bold, but that morning I had seen something in the coating of my mother's eyes. The jaded look of her skin, and the softness in her voice when she told us bye, made me want to clarify what my mother was to him.

He looked startled that I asked but clamped a frown and didn't say anything as he shuffled to his room. Minutes later, he emerged with his arms folded over a rifle. Dad held it up and exposed the chamber so that I could see a round was loaded, then snapped it back and caressed the steel barrel with his fingers. He perched on the edge of the table, then placed the gun in between us, staring straight ahead. My eyes followed his gaze and landed on my sister. She was settled in a recliner, playing with a doll, softly singing to herself. Her voice was sweet, and the words floated innocently from her lips. I glanced back at the rifle that aimed in her direction. He didn't have to explain. I knew my sister was in the crosshairs.

I remember that moment clearly, before he even spoke, when I made the connection. The air felt heavy, wicked. Dad stared at me.

"Put your finger on the trigger," he said calmly.

I shook my head.

He shifted his body and leaned so that his face was only inches from mine. "I'm not telling you again."

Trembling, I placed my finger on the trigger. Fear settled in the air around me as Dad calmly lit a cigarette. He puffed on it for a moment, then put it out. I slid my hand away from the gun.

"If anything happens to your sister, remember it's your fault. You pulled the trigger. Got it?"

I nodded, then he stood, wiped the gun down, and ambled back to his room, toting it under his arm.

I knew that things had changed, much like a chess game I had gotten for Christmas. There were other people in Dad's game now. Lena had somehow managed to become a queen piece. I stared at Gabby, who stopped playing long enough to look up and smile at me. She didn't know it, but over the last fifteen minutes, her value had drastically increased. She had been promoted to pawn, and it was all because I decided to stick my fat neck out and play knight.

My stomach heaving, I made my way to the bathroom and vomited everything I had eaten for lunch.

I'm sure each of my family members has their own memory from this time. Bubba got his first BB gun that year and walked up and down the road with it slung over his shoulder, his eyes sweeping the tree line for some poor bird that wasn't fast enough. Gabby pedaled a red tricycle up and down the driveway almost daily, at times tumbling over, giggling. Mom and Dad were both settling into their new jobs. But in my memory, I was watching the back door, tensely, and Dad was committing statutory rape in the next room with the neighbors' granddaughter.

Chapter 6:

Rat Jabber

That winter was bitter cold, and frost covered the ground most mornings, making it look clean and crisp. The week of Christmas, when Josephine and Jack's parents couldn't make the trip to West Monroe to celebrate with Grandma Avis and Aunt Carol, Dad said the cousins could hitch a ride with us. He explained that there wasn't enough room for everyone in the cab of the truck. Jack, Josephine, Bubba, and I piled into the bed of his pickup truck in thirty-degree weather to make the four-hour drive. Dad said we would be fine—that a little cold air never killed anybody—and told us we had to lay flat on our backs the entire trip. He explained that we were the lucky ones because we could take a nap while he had to drive. We covered and strapped the Christmas gifts near the tailgate. Gabby waved to us from inside the cozy cab as he tossed a blanket on top of us.

At first it wasn't too bad, but once Dad started doing seventy or eighty miles an hour—he liked to speed—the wind whipped the blanket around, and we grasped at it frantically. After a few minutes my fingers felt frozen. I buried my face in Josephine's side, but it did no good. She was just as cold as I was. My teeth started chattering, and Jack yelled at me for making too much noise. Soon everyone else's teeth were chattering too, and Josephine suggested we sing songs to pass the time. After a while, I completely forgot that my knees were knocking together.

Sometimes Dad would hit a big pothole and we all flew up into the air. The bed of the truck was hard and cold, and I felt like we would fly out. After a while, I began to wonder if he was trying to dodge any of the potholes, or if he was speeding up, just before he hit them. Each time he made a turn at an unusually fast speed, we all rolled in one direction or the other like logs. The truck never slowed down, and we continued to sing as we banged down the beaten road to West Monroe.

When we finally stopped at Grandma's house, we had trouble standing and moved around like a small herd of sloths. Bubba was sort of stiff, like a giant exclamation point, so we dragged him to the tailgate where we could ease him off. Dad hollered at us to stop playing around and unload the truck. We leaned Bubba up and loaded as many wrapped presents as we could fit into our arms. Our bones made crackling sounds, like kindling popping in a fire, and we were whiter than ghosts. The packages were intact.

―――

AUNT CAROL WAS SLIDING A HAM in the oven when we entered. The heavenly smell it offered, along with that of freshly baked cookies, drifted through the house while we gathered around the table, drinking hot cocoa, desperately trying to warm up. Wee Dog barked and growled at all our feet as Aunt Carol slipped him treats under the table. The Christmas tree in the living room was decorated with flocked glass balls, colorful baubles shaped like icicles, miniature sequin stockings, and silver tinsel hanging from the branches. Presents were stacked several feet high all around the tree, and we could hardly wait to rip them open.

"I think this might be our biggest haul yet," Josephine said.

Aunt Carol had even more gerbils than she did before—they kept multiplying—so she had sorted them into different cages and named them all. She went on and on about all the daily gerbil activities.

"They didn't come all this way to hear you jabber on about rats. Keep the rat talk to yourself," Grandma muttered.

"Why don't you stop sticking your big fat nose into other people's business?" Aunt Carol shouted.

"My big fat nose has to clean up after these animals all day."

"I'm busy working during the day, Avis. Excuse me if I don't have time to buy you a medal."

"Are you getting another cup of coffee? That must be your sixth cup."

"Yes, it is, and I've needed *every* single one."

I walked over to the big picture window and noticed my younger cousin Tim, who lived in Grandma's house with his mother, sitting in the front ditch, setting a remote-controlled truck on fire. Small flames leapt into the air.

"Hey!" I hollered over my great-aunt Carol and Grandma. "Tim's setting a toy truck on fire. That's the third one since we got here."

"Well, it's his truck," his mom said. "He can do what he wants."

Josephine reached across the table and yanked Jack's hair. He jumped up, startling Wee Dog, who violently snapped at different feet. Josephine vaulted from the table and ran, screaming through the house, with Jack red-faced and hot on her trail.

"I'm so glad Christmas is about peace and unity," I said, but no one seemed to hear. "Can we just open the gifts?" I hollered over the chaos.

My grandmother had another sister who lived in New Orleans and happened to be a millionaire, with no kids of her own. This turned out to be an advantage for all of us. Every Christmas, she sent a big fat check to my grandmother so she could buy Christmas presents for everyone in the family. Aunt Carol and Grandma usually bought us dozens of presents with the money. One gift sitting under the tree for me was large and heavy. I carefully pulled the paper back and opened the box. Inside was the fattest dictionary I'd ever seen in my life.

"Don't you just love it?" Grandma asked, her eyes shining with excitement. "I heard how you like to memorize words, so I thought this would be perfect for you."

Every day, for years, Dad had made Bubba and me memorize words out of a dictionary, just a small, but thick paperback that stayed parked on the dining table. We had to recite twenty words and their full definitions at the end of each week. If we failed at one word, we had to go back and memorize them again, until, without fail, we got them all right. "Grandma," I said, pressing my hand on the blue leathery front, "I love it."

I glanced over at Dad, who was beaming, completely enraptured.

"It's one of those new dictionaries with all the latest words," she said with her hands clasped together.

I remember that Christmas with startling clarity. My grandmother's grinning face, how she had no idea that learning was a traumatic event for me, and I'm quite sure for my brother, too. For extra studying, Dad had bought us two sets of encyclopedias, and two thick math books that taught a condensed version of every type of math, including algebra and calculus.

Four decades later, I keep the dictionary she gave me within reach on my desk. Every so often I slip on a pair of readers and trace my fingers on random definitions, cherishing the Christmas my grandma gifted me a box of words.

By the time all the gifts were opened, Grandma and Aunt Carol were involved in another full-fledged shouting match. Tim was throwing cheese balls all over the living room and stomping on them. Josephine was running through the house again with one of Jack's gifts tucked under her arm as the latter chased behind her, and Wee Dog lunged and snapped at everyone in the kitchen, whether they had feet or not.

That evening, Dad told Bubba and Jack to go ride into town with him. Mom looked at him as though to question him, but Aunt Carol and Grandma started arguing about dog food and Dad slipped out the door with Jack and Bubba. They returned a few hours later, quiet. When Mom asked where they'd been, Dad said they'd just gone sightseeing. I looked over at Bubba and Jack, who had already settled into the living room. They said nothing.

The next day, before we hopped in the back of the truck for the ride home, I gave my grandmother a long hug. "I'm so glad that we came, Grandma."

"Yes, I'm glad you came too. There's just something about Christmas that seems to bring us all closer together."

———

IN THE SEVENTH GRADE, I had to choose an extracurricular activity. I chose band and randomly decided to play the trumpet. It was gold and had two mouthpieces that fit snugly in a brown leather case. I was so good, the band director sent me to the cafeteria, between breakfast and lunch, to practice by myself so the rest of the band wouldn't be jealous of my skills. I was a distraction to the rest of the students, he said, and deserved a special place to play. I never marched with the band or got invited on any trips, either, because my marching skills were above par as well.

There must have been an echo in the cafeteria, because the lunch ladies put cotton balls in their ears whenever I walked in with my trumpet case. The band director gave me an A every day on progress. Once every six weeks, he charged into the cafeteria and told me to play a quick song, then gave the thumbs up and ran back to class, before somebody with a tuba hit somebody with a snare drum.

One day, as he was running out, a lunch lady started chasing him with a rolling pin. "You are going to pay for this!" she screamed.

Thankfully, my parents had saved money buying a used trumpet from the classifieds. After a bacterial infection spread across my face from putting my lips on it, Mom took me to see a doctor. My face almost fell off, but Dad said the seventy-five dollars they saved buying the used one would cover my medical treatment.

As we drove to the dermatologist, I picked at the white crust that was slowly creeping across my face. I noticed a long gray Mercedes parked in the *Reserved for Doctor* space. There were no signs that indicated any spots were reserved for patients, so we parked the Oldsmobile in the empty spot next to the shiny Mercedes.

The doctor had large round glasses, silver hair, and strands of white shooting out of his nose and ears. He wore a white jacket, like all doctors do, and as he held my face, I tried not to look him in the eyes. He squished up his thick eyebrows. They looked like white fuzzy caterpillars. When he handed the prescription to me, I traced his chicken scratch with my fingers. There was not one word I could understand. As he was writing on his chart, I asked him if that was English.

He looked over the round glasses that sat perched on the bridge of his nose. "It's Latin," he said, pushing his glasses further up. He then went back to writing on the chart.

My interest had been captured. I wondered if what he was writing on the chart was in Latin too. I said it over and over in my mind. I knew he drove a Mercedes and had a special spot reserved for him and his car. I reasoned that it must be a language that rich people use. I had Mom take me to the library that weekend, which was our usual haunt. Several Latin books sat on a shelf, and I perused them all. By that weekend, I had a new phrase to stuff in my sole.

Dum vita est spes est.
Where there's life, there's hope.

Chapter 7:

Adopted

By now, we were living high on the hog in a mobile home. Mom and Dad bought new furniture and a new truck with a tinted sliding glass window in the back. Mom declared that we were steadily moving up in the world.

One Saturday, Dad decided that Gabby needed a clubhouse. The neighborhood was full of girls her age. They all ran around with long ponytails and sandals and armloads of Care Bears and Rainbow Brite dolls. Mom agreed with Dad that Gabby should have nice things since she was the youngest. Besides, she told us, Bubba and I had each other and that was something that money couldn't buy. Just months earlier, Dad had custom built her a doll house, furnished from top to bottom. She was now the doting owner of dozens of Barbies that all needed her constant attention. Now his truck made its way once more to the lumber yard.

Dad was no longer working at a plant but had a job as a delivery driver, making double the salary. He had given the company a tale as tall as a giraffe's neck about how he had graduated high school and had plenty of driving experience. They hired him on the spot. When they found out he was lying and that he had dropped out of school in the eighth grade, they threatened to fire him. He spent three days screaming at us and smashing our things. But they let him stay on anyway, so money was not as much of an issue as it was before. The bills still piled up, only not as high.

Dad spent two weekends building a playhouse the size of a small shed, measuring, sawing, cussing, hammering, and painting. Inside, it had shelving for Gabby to place different toys and a seating area for her and her friends. Bubba and I lugged crates of toys and dolls from her room to fill the playhouse. She pointed to where each one went.

We were old enough to earn our keep by tending to the lawn and Dad's vegetable garden on the weekends and after school. Bubba usually mowed the grass, while I trimmed the edging. When we were done, we cleaned out the dog kennel and washed the vehicles before the garden got our attention. The garden was huge with rows of corn, tomatoes, peas, peppers, and carrots. We dropped on our hands and knees, pulling crabgrass, and plucking beetles and caterpillars off the plants. Bubba preferred to squeeze their juicy insides between his fingers, but I tried to save them in a jar and relocate them. On occasion, when I was on my twentieth or thirtieth lap around the trailer, or on my knees pulling weeds in Dad's garden, I'd find myself remembering the love I received from Sarah's family. Something was slowly shattering inside of me. It felt like a woodpecker chipping away at my heart.

Bubba and I spent hours every week pulling weeds as the sun beat down on us, pausing only to wipe our dripping foreheads with the backs of our arms. Through the bony corn stalks and paper leaves, I could make out Gabby and her friends, tromping in and out of the playhouse with armloads of dolls, toys, and small pets. I couldn't help but notice that Dad hadn't forced her to memorize parts of the Declaration of Independence, memorize the dictionary, write one hundred-page reports, or jog a mile every day. He also hadn't tossed her into a wall or punched her in the face.

The difference in how Gabby was treated, compared to us, was so stark, one of the neighbors asked me if Bubba and I were adopted.

MY BODY STARTED CHANGING and, one day, two large bumps appeared on my chest. At first, I was concerned, then Mom said I needed to start wearing a bra. My friend Anita also got bumps on her chest, so her mom got her a bra too. One Saturday, I brought Anita over to work on a science project with me. When Dad saw Anita, he was enraptured. His eyes stayed fixed on Anita when I introduced her. Mom went to her room to read a book, while Anita and I went to my room. When I went to close the door, Dad appeared. He was grinning from ear to ear. He asked Anita if she wanted anything to drink. She told him she didn't. He placed his hand on her shoulder and squeezed, "Let me know if you need anything."

Anita nodded; it was several moments before Dad removed his hand and walked away.

The next day at school, Anita said, "Did you see how your dad was staring at me yesterday?"

"No, how?"

"Like I was some kind of prey."

I shrugged.

"I don't know how you didn't notice," she said. "It was *so* obvious. To be honest, he was staring at you that way too." She made a face of disgust. I didn't say anything. I hadn't noticed.

That Friday night, I was half asleep when my bedroom door squeaked open. Light from the hallway cut through my room. I glanced at the light. Dad appeared, nude. He made his way around my bed to where I lay. His eyes were dark, as though they had been colored in with shadows. I'd never seen pupils so dilated; the blackness bulldozed straight out of his soul, an abandoned tunnel of infinite void. The room felt strangely heavy, suffocating, and I winced at the suddenness of it all. Dad pressed his hands on my chest. I started to let out a scream, but he quickly clamped his hand over my mouth and whispered to me not to wake anyone. He said that Mom had sent him so he could teach me how to be a woman. Once again, I tried to scream, and he jammed his hand on my windpipe. I could feel my eyes trying to squeeze out of their sockets. I slowly started to suffocate.

"Do you understand?" He loosened his hold on my neck.

I caught my breath and wheezed, "I'll fight you for the rest my life."

"I'd kill you right now," Dad snarled, gripping my throat, pressing my windpipe once more. "But I'd have to get dressed and find a place to get rid of your worthless body."

He released his hold on me and left as I lay, gulping pockets of air. He came back numerous times throughout the night, cussing at me, filling my room with hot whiskey breath. He was hoping I would be asleep, but I lay in the bed, staring at the ceiling all night, waiting for him. Each time I told him to leave me alone. He gripped my throat so that I could scarcely breathe.

I stayed awake the following night, listening for the creak of the door. I heard the whirr of the blender as he made Mom daiquiris. Around midnight, she ambled to her room. I mentally prepared myself for what was to come. I'd left my door cracked so I could see him coming down the hall. After half an hour or so, the floor leading down the hall slowly creaked. I gazed at Dad's shadow that the nightlight cast on the hallway wall. The shadow slowly crept, completely unaware that I was watching it.

My eyes stayed riveted on the door. When it began to slowly open, I closed my eyes pretending to be asleep. Within moments, his hands were feeling on my chest, then he started cussing. I had outsmarted him. Underneath my nightgown, I was wearing a sweat suit and several T-shirts. That afternoon I had asked my mom for some patchwork quilts she had hand-sewn; they were neatly folded in a linen closet. My room was cold, I told her. I toted them to my room and neatly laid them one by one on my bed, on top of my comforter. When Dad realized that his hands were full of fabric and batting, he tried to pull the quilts up, but my hands held them tightly underneath. He gripped my throat, but I didn't give in. This happened off and on throughout the night—he kept trying to catch me asleep—until he left the room for good, and I absolutely knew he wasn't coming back. Early the next morning, after everyone in the house was awake, he burst through my doorway and told me I was lazy and shouted for me to get out. I nodded as he walked out the room, then I noticed I was soaking wet. Between the quilts and the extra clothing, I was drenched in sweat.

He returned several nights throughout the week. I wiped beads of sweat from my forehead as I waited in the darkness. After midnight, it was hard to stay awake, and sometimes I would drift off. He caught on to my layered clothing tactic, so he'd crank up the heat. My door didn't lock, but I would always close it and even tried putting something in front of it, like a shoe, so that when I woke, I could see if it had moved during the night. Usually, the shoe was pushed away from the door. Sometimes the door had been reclosed, other times not. He always got angry when I did this, and he would tell me to go weed the garden, or find something to do somewhere else, so he wouldn't have to see me.

I spent my weekends wandering for miles. I found a giant sinkhole in a forest and would sit in it sometimes, or even doze on a pile of leaves. One day, I realized that I was a fish in a bowl when I sat in the sinkhole, and if some creep found me there, I would be trapped. I stopped sitting in the sinkhole.

I was exhausted from lack of sleep and could barely drag myself to school. Throughout the day, I yawned my way from class to class. My grades started to suffer as a result, and people called me Lazy Tracie. Teachers just shook their heads as they walked past my desk. I became so tired that I mastered the art of sleeping behind an open book.

Sometimes I would pretend to be sick at school so I could go home and rest my eyes. Mom caught on to my napping scheme and told me she was not going to keep checking me out of school. I wanted to tell her about what was going on, right under her nose, but I couldn't trust her not to tell Dad. He had already threatened to kill everyone if I told. I also didn't believe she would help me. If she couldn't see that something was bothering me, I felt I shouldn't have to tell her.

One day, I was at home, and a movie called *The Great Escape* came on the TV. It was about a group of prisoners at a WWII concentration camp who tried to outwit their German captors. I was drawn into the movie with such intensity that I grabbed a notebook and started scribbling down notes and ideas. From that day on, I was focused on escaping to a better life. I called my plan Operation Great Escape. It renewed my determination to move forward, to keep walking with the papers in my shoes. To dream of a life without Dad sneaking in my room every night. He'd been trying to wear me down for years, but it had always backfired on him. I began to wonder if he'd miscalculated just how much fight was left in me.

THERE WERE EVENINGS WHEN Dad would make me sit on his lap as we watched television in the living room. I was fourteen years old. I'd sit frozen, not wanting to move as a calloused hand crept around my waist. One evening, Mom's eyes darted back and forth between the TV and Dad. Finally, she blurted, "Isn't she a bit old to be sitting in your lap? She doesn't even look comfortable." Dad hollered back at Mom that it was my choice, then shoved me onto the floor and pushed me away with his foot. Humiliated, I stood up and slid past them both as I ambled my way to my bedroom. *Has Mom noticed that something is wrong? Will she do something about it?* That question would be answered by the next day because the subject was never brought up again. A few nights later, Dad told me to sit in his lap again. I glanced at Mom to see if she would say something, but she was buried in a book and didn't seem to notice.

As a teenager, I read the *Wall Street Journal* at the library but now also had thick stacks of magazines tucked under my bed, like *Fortune* and *World*

News Report. I sent away for free issues, and they kept sending more, hoping I'd pay for a subscription one day. On the nights that my father assaulted my mother and ravaged our home, I pulled an issue out with a flashlight. With the sounds of violence in the background, I disappeared underneath the cotton armor of bed sheets and quilts.

My parents didn't battle. It was more of a slaughter. Mom never fought back. Dad told her she was weak, and she must have believed it. Dad started coming home later and later Friday nights, until it became almost Saturday morning. Mom would stay up, waiting, her legs folded underneath her, until his pickup slid in the driveway. We all braced when we heard the gravel crunching beneath his tires. Everyone knew what was about to happen. The later he came home was better for me, because it meant he might pass out after he beat Mom.

One morning, Mom saw a broken pool stick behind the seat of his truck and asked him what he had done, but he told her to mind her own business. I noticed a laceration above his eye. It was obvious Dad had been involved in some type of bar brawl. After that, he started drifting in earlier on Friday nights and went right back to sneaking into my room again. I figured somebody had finally given Dad a taste of his own medicine and he hadn't liked it.

Chapter 8:

The Battlefield

———

I awoke to what sounded like a freight train blowing through our mobile home. A resounding boom followed. I could hear my rock necklace swinging violently on its little hook, the steady *tap* it made each time it hit the shelving near my bed. I pulled a blanket over my head and gripped the edges of my mattress. I heard the unmistakable sound of chairs being violently thrown. Broken. The vibrations from my parents' running shook the trailer so much, it moaned and groaned and lurched as though it were going to dismantle itself. I didn't have to see what was happening to know Dad was drunk.

My door burst open, and Mom flipped the light switch. I bolted up. Her face was distorted and bent in an odd way, and blood streamed from her nose and mouth. She was panting. I bit my lip at the sight of her bloodstained teeth and shirt. She stretched her arm across my bed and wheezed my name. I was only able to clasp her hand for a moment, before Dad stormed in the room, eyes bulging, and ripped our hands apart.

I have flashbacks of this memory more than any other. It plays in my head over and over again like a montage. Mom, who wouldn't hurt a fly if it landed on her, standing at my bed with her white clothes soaked in blood. Dad, still in his brown delivery uniform Mom had so carefully starched that morning, closing in over her, with not a drop of blood, nor a scratch on him. He was tan and muscular, pressed. She was pale, her face already starting to warp and twist, the skin around her eyes already tinting a pale lilac. For only seconds, they were both staring at me at the exact same time, unmoving, like a still frame. Mom's face was a frozen desperate plea. Dad's face was fire, his blue eyes glassy like pools of water. A vein in his neck bulged as he glared at me, zigzagging downward, a swollen, feral river.

When triggered, my mind has often played this scene in a loop. I wanted to help my mother, wanted to do more than extend my hand. The entire room in these moments told a story. My rock necklace continued to click the seconds away. The horse statues I had arranged all over my room stood like stage props. My hamster stopped cramming food in his mouth long enough to be a character in a clip that didn't want to end. Those five seconds were an eternity before the set scene seamlessly dissolved. Dad grabbed a large clump of Mom's hair and yanked her out of the room. My necklace ticked faster against the shelf. I didn't remove it. I knew when the necklace stopped, my mother would be either unconscious or dead.

His voice was violent and booming, hysterical, shouting that he was going to bury her that night, but she was going to suffer first. Blood was smeared on my light switch. I watched as veins of crimson slowly trailed down my wall in an irregular pattern. I realized my hand was wet. I held it up and twisted it in the light, watching blood drip down my wrist. I took a pair of dark socks out of my drawer and wiped my hand and the wall clean. Mom's screams blurred into an endless cry throughout our home. I closed my eyes and clutched the bloody socks to my chest as I rocked back and forth on my bed. The noise went on for over half an hour before I heard one final violent *thud* and then all noises stopped.

———

BY THREE O'CLOCK IN the morning, I hadn't heard anything for a while, and I was certain Dad had passed out. It had been a particularly violent night. I swung my legs out of bed and slipped on a pair of slippers. I walked to my door, and pulled it open quietly. I crept down the hall, searching for my mother, just to make sure he hadn't killed her. If he had, I'd leave with Bubba and Gabby. There was no use in waiting for him to kill us too.

Nightlights cast small shadows across the living room. Shards of glass glittered, exhibiting my dad's wrath like sparkling diamonds. It was the usual scene, a visual narrative documenting a late-night fight. I saw a large knife my mother used to cut meat stuck in a wall, eye-level with me, where it had landed after he flung it at her. With both hands, I grasped the handle and jiggled. It was that moment, when I yanked the cold steel out the wall, that I felt the first shift in my childhood, when I felt veins of cortisol surge through my body, *when I'd had enough*. I peered at the edge of the knife, then toward his bedroom.

I clung to the handle and held it at my side. I inched my way through the living room and across the kitchen floor, careful not to step on the blood that had dripped and splattered from my mother while she ran for her life. Objects he'd chucked across the room lay flipped or scattered on the floor. As I crept out the kitchen, into the second hallway, an otherworldly darkness arose within me—the kind that only a bottomless chasm can harbor, pitching my mind into an abyss I'd never ventured before. Any good thoughts I had before I pulled the knife out the wall shredded into the abyss.

Gabby's room was to the left, just before theirs. Sometimes she slept with me, but not tonight. I peeked in. My Little Ponies and Care Bears were neatly lined up on a shelf. A nightlight cast a soft glow on her face as she hugged a doll. Gabby was the only one in our home who wasn't part of the madness. My parents adored her. She wanted for nothing, and great care was given by each of us to shield her from the pain.

When I saw her, I let out quiet sobs and put my hand over my mouth. I wanted to destroy him for everything he'd done to us. I wanted him perfectly destroyed, and I wanted to be the one to do it. I shook my head from left to right, to knock some sense into it, and let the knife fall to the carpet. It wouldn't be me who destroyed him. At least, not that night.

It was a moment of realization for me. Grandma Avis had once told me that Dad was beaten as a child. She said that no matter how badly Dad treated us sometimes, he had been treated worse. Of course, it didn't make me feel any better. Grandma didn't know how badly we lived. She was two hundred miles away.

Please don't let me kill him.

Even though decades have passed since the incident, my brain gets easily triggered by the breaking of a glass or a spotting of blood. It drags me back to that moment in my childhood, when I stood breathless, staring at the battlefield my dad had singlehandedly created.

THE NEXT MORNING, WHEN I saw my mother, I gasped. Her face had ballooned to at least twice its normal size, so swollen I felt it might pop. It looked like a baby elephant head, purple beyond recognition. Her eyes were just thin lines, her forehead and cheeks puffed up and overshadowing them. She looked oddly like a caricature with a comical fleshiness. I thought I was dreaming. I searched her elephant face, trying to recognize her.

"What are you staring at?" she snapped. She put her hand up to her swollen, purple lips, obviously in pain.

I went to my room to get my schoolbooks. I heard her shuffling in the living room and kitchen, trying to clean up everything he'd smashed or broken the night before. Eventually, I came out of my room to help, but I couldn't stomach looking at her. She moved slowly, with care. I picked up things without speaking. She had some cracked ribs, but she wouldn't go to the doctor because they ask questions. Dad didn't like questions.

A few days later, she said that we had to go to the store down the road for a few supplies. I looked at her contorted purple face, the black rings around her eyes, the burst blood vessels, and the way she walked hunched over in pain. I was already treated as an outcast at school; this would trigger an entire new barrage of insults if anyone saw us together.

"Please," I begged, "can't it wait?"

"No," she mumbled. "We are running out of things. Life still goes on."

When we were at the store, I didn't stay at her side like I normally did. I sneaked behind clothing racks and endcaps of merchandise, at one point hiding my face behind a box of cereal, certain someone would know we were together. Mom told me to stop hiding and help her check out her items. Since I hadn't seen anyone who I knew from my school, I felt it was safe. As I was loading the items onto the counter at the checkout, the doorbell clanged. I looked up to see two girls from my class, staring at my mother, jaws hanging. I stepped back to make it appear as though I wasn't with her. I glanced sideways at Mom, who was slowly pushing her items onto the counter, and pretended to be in shock at this beat-up woman in front of me. They both appraised me, then Mom, before walking away.

When we got in the car, I blurted out, "You embarrassed me. Why did you have to be seen out in public? Why can't you go to the store by yourself? He's going to beat you anyway." I regretted saying it almost immediately.

Mom never said extraordinary things and got confused easily—she once told someone that I had a blood transplant instead of a blood transfusion—but had a way of staring into you, to reveal what was on her mind, when she was at a loss for words. This was one of those times. She didn't say anything and spent a minute just staring blankly out the windshield, occasionally reaching up to touch her puffy cheeks. Then she shifted the car in reverse and pulled out of her space. She was silent for the ride home. When we slipped into the driveway, she let out a sigh, before she turned and looked at me, squinting through her raccoon eyes as if to say, *Don't worry, I'm going to fix this.*

THE NEXT EVENING, WHEN I got home from school, my mother's pain had not subsided, but had, in fact, gotten worse. Despite that, she had heaved suitcases onto the bed. She told us to pack all our clothes into the car. We jammed everything that would fit. There was nothing left in our closets but a few wire hangers.

At first, I wanted to celebrate, but this idea was quickly snuffed out by fear. We'd done this before. Left him, came back. Left him, came back. I wished we had a place to go that was secret. He knew we always fled to my grandmother's and within twenty-four hours ended up going back. Because Bubba and I "participated," we always got punished afterward.

The drive to my grandmother's house was a long one. Mom was slumped in the seat trying to see over the steering wheel. Occasionally, she would let out a moan. She seemed to be getting worse. I stared out the rear window, watching the road wind up and down behind us, like a dark ribbon.

The next morning, he was knocking on my grandmother's door. Fully contrite, begging, sweetly pleading loudly enough that I was sure several neighbors could hear. Grandma was terrified and told him so. She begged him to leave. I saw her shaking.

"Come on, Avis, let me in. I'm sorry for what I did. Let me in," he begged.

"I'm scared of you," she told him through the closed door.

"I won't hurt you; I promise. Go tell her I'm here and want to speak to her."

Aunt Carol was pacing, shaking her head, muttering that he was crazy and should go to jail.

Grandma Avis talked to my mom, who agreed she would speak with him. Every time her chest rose, she winced in pain.

"This is a bad idea," Aunt Carol told Grandma.

"I don't know what else to do," Grandma answered. She looked over at me. "Tracie, you and Bubba take Gabby and go hide in a bedroom. If something happens, run for help."

I silently nodded as Bubba and I looked for a place to hide. We hid in a closet of clothes and shoe boxes with our ears pressed to the door, wondering what Dad would say to Mom. Wondering if Mom would give in to Dad. We heard heavy footsteps. Things got quiet for about thirty seconds, and I thought perhaps he had decided to leave Mom alone. Maybe we could stay.

Two minutes later, I heard Mom's suitcases snapping shut, then footsteps marching away. I left Bubba and Gabby and sprinted to check on her. Mom struggled to sit, then perched on the edge of the mattress, her hand placed on her ribcage. She gasped for breath and let out a slight moan. "Get your things, we're going home," she said.

"Mom," I whispered, as Dad carried her suitcases out to the car, "are you sure you're up to this? You need to go to a hospital."

"Just get in the car," she snapped.

Aunt Carol was fit to be tied. She was bustling about the living room, muttering to herself, gathering the rest of our things together, before finally shouting, "What just happened?"

Mom pushed past Aunt Carol, her left hand clamped to her side, her back hooked and eyes cast downward, not saying a thing. Absorbed by the grim moment, we all quietly stood watching her shuffle across the room. Someone dropped a glass, and I almost jumped out of my skin. In the muted stillness of the room, it may as well have been a missile that dropped. Mom continued to press forward. I found myself shaking my head from left to right, trying to knock some sense in it. It was time to leave.

I sat in the passenger seat with my arms crossed as we followed behind Dad's truck. We drove past timber companies, where stacks of jumbo logs were piled on top of each other, forming giant wooden pyramids along the side of the road. When a logging truck got in between our car and his truck, Dad pulled over, until we were in his view again, then he jumped back in front of us, his eyes constantly glancing to the rearview mirror to make sure we hadn't disappeared.

I kept my eyes fastened on Gabby, who was riding in Dad's truck and occasionally turned to look out the back window and wave to us. I felt like Dad was using Gabby as bait to make sure we didn't try to escape. "I don't know why we have to go back," I complained. "You always give in to him."

"I'm not giving in," my mother said through clenched teeth.

"Then why are we going back?"

She said nothing but studied the road. I gazed at her while I waited for a reply. Her face had deflated some over the last few days, but it still looked as though it was full of hot air and might float away on a strong breeze.

Several minutes passed before she replied. "He told me he had a loaded shotgun in his truck, and he was going to shoot everyone in the house if I didn't go back. Does that answer your question?"

A chilling hush settled in the car; the engine hummed quietly as we continued traveling. I shifted in my seat.

"Yes." I said it like I was ashamed for having asked.

She drove in silence for the rest of the trip. I didn't need elaboration. Dad was using the same threats on Mom as he had on me. They worked for him. He didn't have to change his script. He had professionally written a one-act feature film, starring himself as the main actor. Mom and I were the supporting actresses, a gun was the prop, and the scenes played in a loop, indefinitely.

When we finally arrived home and Bubba and I got out of the car, Dad stopped us before we could go inside. "Not you two. Since you like to encourage your mother to run away, go to the back garden and pull crabgrass and pick bugs off the plants. That should keep you busy for at least three or four hours. As a matter of fact, I don't want to see either of you for the rest of the day. Stay out of my sight." Then he opened the door to gently help Mom out and guide her up the steps.

Drained emotionally and physically from the trip, Bubba and I trudged to the backyard, plopped down on our hands and knees, and started pulling weeds. Before long, I had a small jar of mushy green captives ready to be relocated. I stared at the bugs inside this jar and wondered if they even knew they weren't free.

I decided to name them, like Aunt Carol named her gerbils and wild mice. "Hi, Nibbles. Hi, Slimey. Hi, Twiggy," I said as I wiped the sweat dripping from my forehead. "You'll be free soon, just somewhere else."

After a while, the back door flung open, and Dad leaned across the back steps to wring out a wet mop. Moments later, a bucket of dirty mop water was tossed out. It was then that I recognized just how awkward and disturbed our life was, that the good things and bad things danced on a fine, fine line. I couldn't pretend to understand it, and I can't say I wanted to. All I knew was this: When life beats the hell out of you, it will also turn around and mop up the mess.

CHAPTER 9:

LION

—

A muddy bayou, as brown and thick as gumbo, snaked its way through the new town we were living in. On a humid Saturday morning, I decided to forge my way through overgrowth, pushing aside branches and logs, until I reached its edge. A thin fog hovered above it, which made it look haunted by misty ghosts. Egrets with spindly legs swaggered along the edge, spearing crawfish with their long bills, only stopping to stare at me for a moment, before realizing the crustaceans were of more interest. Huge oak limbs spread across the water, slicing through the fog.

It was on this walk that I stumbled on an old, abandoned clapboard house, hidden in a copse off the water's edge, and claimed it as my own. The paint was weathered on the outside, worn down to an ashen gray. Most of the windows were broken, and the tin roof almost rusted through. Poison ivy scaled the sides, hiding the rot and decay underneath.

Inside was worse. Rusty appliances, a sagging cot with a ratty blanket, hundreds of smashed beer cans and empty whiskey bottles scattered across the faded plank floors. It was invaded by mold, snakes—shed skins were the evidence—and all sorts of vegetation. Now it was mine.

I decided to spruce it up. For weeks, I spent evenings after school, sweeping with an old corn broom I found in a closet. I snuck some garbage bags from home and filled them with all the bottles and cans. Then I decided to sneak some more things, like a sheet of plastic to fit over the cot, a cheap itchy blanket that wouldn't be missed, snacks, and a poster of a golden palomino that I taped to one of the walls.

There was no electricity, so I had to rely completely on natural sunlight, which filtered through the cracks and windows. To dress up the outside, I fetched a compact shovel and transplanted some wildflowers along the edges of the rotting steps. I borrowed a paintbrush and some paint from my dad's shed to put fresh paint on the window frames.

When I was done, I stood outside in complete satisfaction, admiring my work. I knew this wasn't a real home, but it was a place to get away. I wrote a new note and placed it in my sneaker. *I want a place to call home.*

I put that dream in my shoe and walked on it until the paper was rubbed blank. I walked the words right off. I often imagined Bubba and me in a better place. In a real home with people who loved us. But that didn't seem like it was going to happen fast enough. Dad was careful not to leave any fingerprints as proof of his crimes, at least not on me. He did leave blood stripes across my brother's legs, but no one seemed to notice. I realized that men were harder on boys. It was expected for them to be as tough as meat. I watched as a hardness began to crust over Bubba, how his personality began to shift. There were days his eyes seemed to glaze over. I felt like I was losing him. And I was. The clapboard house was my secret escape from everything, and little by little, I pushed my brother from my mind.

At times, I lay on the old cot and read a book. The characters in the books, as always, swept me to faraway places. The worlds in the books casually stripped the darkness from mine, layer by layer, until all I could see was hope. They sucked the thickness out of the air and ripped the gray right out of the clouds. Each day that my life felt heavier and oppressed, I picked up a book and crawled into the safety of its pages. I hoped that one day my life would be like all the lives in the books—fated for a happy ending.

———

FOR MY THIRTEENTH BIRTHDAY, I asked my parents for a Badge-A-Minit button press. I devised a plan to run away, and the money I got from the sale of buttons would help bankroll my escape. Each day I practiced different designs and drawings and would cut my designs with a circle cutter that came with the press. Then I would put the different pieces of the button, along with the cut design, in the press and smash everything together, with all my might.

One day I wore several buttons to school and people crowded around me, asking me where I got them. When I told them that I made buttons, word spread like wildfire. Soon, I had over a hundred orders for buttons at one dollar apiece. Some kids wanted buttons, saying who they loved or what they liked, or even showing school spirit. Then the sports coaches approached me about making buttons for the football and baseball games.

Pretty soon, I had orders for hundreds of game buttons. The coaches would cut me checks and then sell the buttons at a higher cost at the games. After Mom cashed the checks for me, I stashed the money in a plastic box I had on a shelf and watched my running-away reserve grow every week. I didn't know when it would happen, but I knew that one day, it would. Timing was everything.

―

IN 1755, AN EVENT known as *Le Grand Dérangement* forced thousands of French people from their homes in Nova Scotia, Canada, for refusing to renounce their Catholic beliefs and convert to the Anglican Church. Their homes and crops burning in the background, these people left with only what they could carry, fleeing to the sea in such horrible conditions, that more than half would lose their lives in the attempt. The survivors would be allowed to settle in southern Louisiana, along bayous and small waterways. They would come to be known as Cajuns, living in an area called Acadiana, which is where my family now lived.

My ninth-grade civics teacher, Mr. LeBlanc, had an exotic accent—a mixture of French and a Southern drawl—and called himself a Cajun. Not only that, but he was also our cool teacher, the kind who high-fived you in the hall, rolled his eyes when the principal walked by, and didn't make a big deal if you were caught cheating in class. Plus, I think he knew our school sucked at being a school.

I looked forward to his class every day. He was a firm teacher and kept us in line, but he had a devilish grin and jaunty sense of humor that made us want to have his respect, so we listened in hushed silence.

Since the incident with Dad, Anita hardly talked to me anymore, so I often leaned up against a brick wall at recess. In elementary school, wearing cheap clothes and no makeup wasn't as obvious, but in high school it got you tortured. My parents seemed to be especially frugal when buying clothes for Bubba and me. Mom even sewed different colored paisley bandannas into square shirts for me to wear.

Each day, Mr. LeBlanc seemed to go out of his way to say hello to me. Life had become so dark and bleak, that sometimes it would feel as though a supermassive black hole would appear beneath me, swirling underneath my feet. I pictured myself as just a particle of material, hovering over the abyss of my life. Mr. LeBlanc's smile was a harness dropped from the heavens that I could grab hold of and dangle from, swinging on the cusp of a swirling disc of dark matter, as gravity tried to pull me down.

One afternoon, while I was sitting on a set of steps reading and waiting for the bus, Mr. LeBlanc cheerfully walked up to me. "How's it going, Tracie? Are you studying for my test tomorrow?"

"No, Mr. LeBlanc. I already know all the answers." He made learning enjoyable and was the only positive influence in my life. I inhaled every word he said.

"Well, that's my star student."

"Mr. LeBlanc?"

"Yes?"

"You've been teaching here a long time, right?"

"Yes. I guess you're implying that I'm old," he said with an impish laugh, and placed a gentle hand on my shoulder.

I froze when he touched me, forgetting where I was going with the conversation. It was as if lightning had struck me where he placed his hand. I wasn't used to being touched by a man, other than my dad. Mr. LeBlanc gaped at me for about half a minute, as if wondering what was going on inside my head. My voice only croaked some incoherent words before he walked off.

I stared across the street at a small store people were bustling in and out of. It was time I got away from Dad.

SOME OF THE TEACHERS at my school were strange and hated the students for making them be there. My math teacher, Mr. Schultz, was one of those. He was a balding and angry math machine, with a large bulbous nose. He was old, and he was also completely bananas. For some reason, he was under the impression that I wanted to master reciprocals. There weren't enough reciprocals in the world to make me want to impress Mr. Schultz. He fully believed that he was God's gift to variables and relished the fact that he could bore us to death with them. I usually just sat with my arms crossed, paying little attention.

His side passion was making fun of kids in the class. One boy had failed the year before, and his name was Jason ReDoe. Mr. Schultz called him Jason Redo because, "he liked to repeat things." Mr. Schultz told Jason he would probably spend the rest of his life in the ninth grade. For some reason, he always called me "Stacy," and also sometimes "Lion," because my hair puffed out on the sides, like a lion's mane.

"Okay, I'm stuck here, teaching the lot of you how to do basic math," he said, even though we were taking algebra. "I'll show you just one time. You either catch on, or you fail my class. Is that understood?"

"Yes, Mr. Schultz," we all said in unison.

One day, he grabbed a piece of chalk and wrote a difficult algebra problem on the blackboard. "I want to see how many of you actually pay attention. Who can come up here and solve this equation?"

No one raised their hand.

"Mr. Redo? How about you?"

Everyone looked over at Jason, who shook his head and cast his eyes downward.

Mr. Schultz snickered and then focused on me. I shifted in my seat.

"How about you, Lion?"

Just like Jason, I shook my head.

"I bet Lion couldn't even solve one plus one," he jabbed, and the class erupted in laughter. "Let's see if she can." He turned to the blackboard and wrote *1+1=* next to the algebra equation. Turning back to the class, he walked to my desk, held the chalk out to me, and told me to go to the board and try to solve it.

I took the chalk from his hand and trudged up to the blackboard. Underneath *1+1=* I wrote a *3*. I turned around, so Mr. Schultz could see.

"Well, I see you proved my point," he said flatly. "Dumb as a brick."

"I'm not finished," I said.

I turned back to the blackboard and sidestepped to the algebra equation he wanted solved. Within seconds, I had it solved and drew a giant box around the answer for emphasis. He was still standing by my desk. I ambled toward him and when I got closer, tossed the stick of chalk in the air. He stretched his hand out to grab it.

"My name is not Lion," I told him. "It's Tracie."

His jaw dropped and a blast of hot air surged at me. "Get out of my class, *Tracie*," he said through gritted teeth. "Go to the office."

I shrugged and grabbed my books. "No problem."

The principal's secretary was busy on a phone call and barely acknowledged me when I walked into the office. Through an open door, I saw the principal, Mr. Knox, signing a stack of papers. I sat down on the wooden bench and pulled out a novel to read while I waited. After a few moments,

I glanced up and saw the principal, motioning to me with his sausage fingers. I put my book down and walked in, ready to receive disciplinary action of some sort.

"Are you the student aide? What took you so long?"

I shrugged, not sure where this was going, but open to where it might lead. I could be whatever he thought I was. Mr. Knox was short, overweight, and reminded me of Boss Hogg from *The Dukes of Hazzard*. He always wore white shirts, and the buttons struggled to confine his wide girth. This was my first time in his office. One wall was framed with newspaper articles about the football team, and another displayed various certificates and awards one gets while being a principal of a school with the winningest team around.

There were only two things that mattered in our town: award-winning sausage and cheese bread made at the locally owned grocery store, and high school football.

Mr. Knox held up a small stack of papers. "Can you bring these papers to the copy room? I need fifty of each. Thank you, this is a big help. I've been needing this done and don't have time to go myself."

At first, I was confused, but then suddenly it was as clear as day. He was senile. I grabbed the papers, smiled, and started to walk off, wondering if he even knew my name was either Stacy or Tracie. I answered to both.

"Wait, one more thing," he called.

I turned, still expecting to be reprimanded for walking out of class, but he pulled out some change from his desk. "Swing by the teacher's lounge and grab yourself a soda and whatever else you'd like. Grab me one too." He dropped a handful of quarters into my hand, along with a principal's hall pass.

On my way out, I grabbed my book so I could read it in the copy room. Walking down the hall, I passed Mr. Schultz's classroom. Seeing me, he shouted my name—Stacy—so I quickly backed up to the open doorway and flashed him the principal's pass. He smiled and crossed his arms triumphantly as he watched me walk off, thinking I was going to a firing squad. I'm not sure what he said to the class, but they erupted in laughter again. I didn't care. *Stacy* was getting a soda while they were all still trying to figure out how she solved that equation.

The lounge was a mysterious place, like a secret fortress for teachers. Two teachers sat in a back corner, each to themselves, reading newspapers.

They glanced up, as if to question me, but I held up the pass, and they went back to their papers. A curl of smoke was winding upward from one of them, as he pulled a cigarette up to his lips and inhaled. He puckered his lips and lazily blew smoke rings into the air, glancing over momentarily to see if I was impressed.

I was.

The sodas felt cool and refreshing in my hands. I licked my lips in anticipation of feeling carbonation ooze down my throat. Now I was ready for the copy room. I drank my soda as the copier spat out page after page. It didn't take as long as I had hoped to make the copies, but I spent the remainder of the hour running errands for the principal.

―――

A FEW DAYS LATER, Jack and Josephine were visiting at the house with their mother. Josephine sat on the edge of my bed, perusing through some books, when Dad appeared in the doorway of my room, giggling. "You know what would be funny?" he whispered loudly to Josephine.

"What?" she asked.

He held out a prescription bottle of pills. "If you lie on the floor and act unconscious with the bottle of pills in your hand, and I'll go tell your mom you committed suicide. It'll be a riot!" he laughed.

Josephine, who was always searching for ways to get back at her mom for different punishments, thought it was a great idea.

I leaned my back against my pillows and crossed my arms. "I'm not in this."

Dad made a face at me and turned his attention back to Josephine. "Act dead," he told her and rushed out the room. Josephine stretched her body onto the floor and tossed the bottle next to her. Within moments, her mom let out a scream and rushed into my room. She grabbed Josephine and started crying, begging her to live, telling her that she loved her. Josephine didn't respond. Tears slid down Aunt Sue's face as she caressed my cousin. She shouted for someone to call an ambulance. Dad couldn't take it anymore and started howling with laughter. "You should have seen the look on your face!" he shouted.

Aunt Sue looked confused.

Josephine, still cradled in her mom's arms, popped her eyes open and said, "Hello, Mommy dearest!"

Aunt Sue's face blanched, and she dropped Josephine. She stood up to confront Dad. "How could you do this to me?" she shouted.

Dad, still laughing, told her it was just a joke. Josephine was rolling on the floor, holding her sides, in a fit of laughter. Mom shook her head and walked off. I sat expressionless on my bed, chewing my bottom lip as the screaming match between Dad and my aunt continued. Even amid the chaos, the only thing I could wonder was: *Had that been me, would my mom have caressed my face like that?*

I WAS STILL FOCUSED on Operation Great Escape and spent a great deal of time plotting how I could make it work. Another part of my plan was to dumb myself down, hoping a teacher would notice the drastic change in my grades and call the police to investigate. I had seen some movie where a student did so horribly in school that his teachers had the parents investigated, and he and his siblings were safely removed and relocated to a safer place. I figured Dad couldn't blame me for snitching if a teacher reported it, and that way, no one would get shot.

So, when my school took the California Achievement Tests, I purposefully answered the questions—hundreds of them—wrong, and in every class. One day, Mr. LeBlanc got back the CAT scores for his history class. He always smiled when I walked into the room. He frowned when I didn't do well on his tests, but he didn't belittle me, and he certainly didn't bully me, like Mr. Schultz did. At first, I didn't know what to think of him. When I realized he was real and embodied what I wished for in a father, not a teacher, I was drawn to him like a bug to a light.

As he walked from desk to desk, handing out the CAT results, he read them—some out loud, some to himself. Sometimes he spoke in Cajun French, and we all laughed. He blithely walked over to my desk with a giant smile on his face, but as he read my results quietly to himself, I watched his mouth melt into a frown. Somehow, he had caught on to my ploy. He didn't say a thing, whether in English or French.

He hovered over me, trying to understand the results. My face turned red as I looked down at years of penciled graffiti on my desk. At some point, somebody named Anna had loved somebody named Jay and had etched it into the soft wood. Out of nervousness, I was now rubbing my thumb against the message. I hadn't wanted to let him down. He was my favorite teacher. But I couldn't let his test be the only one that I passed.

He didn't put the results down on my desk. Instead, he arched his thick black eyebrows and motioned for me to follow him. I walked past the stares and chuckles of my classmates. Someone tossed a wadded-up paper at my back, but I didn't turn to see who. They were all guilty.

I followed him into a room across the hall that looked like a basement. He closed the door behind us. Coppery pipes created a labyrinth on the ceiling. There was a loud humming coming from somewhere. A single light bulb dangled, lit like a dying star, from a wire near an exposed pipe. I could hear the echo of dripping water.

Obviously frustrated, he ran his hands through his hair and asked, "What's wrong? There's something, I know it. You aren't crazy or dumb. You're one of the smartest students I have. Why are you doing this?" He held the results in front of my face. "It is impossible to score all zeros on this test unless you do it on purpose. Impossible, Tracie. What's going on?"

His face went from pale to a light shade of red, as we stared at each other. I opened my mouth, wordless, and started to sob. This was my chance, the chance I'd been waiting for, but I didn't know what to do. What if I told him and he didn't help me? I'd go home to get beaten, then watch Bubba get beaten, because it would certainly be taken out on him as well. I'd watch my dad punish everyone because I'd spoken of the things that happened in our home. Then we'd all float our separate ways in shark-infested waters, and it would be my fault.

Drip. Drip. Drip.

Underneath the dripping, someone had placed a bucket, and it was ready to overflow. I had never been in this room, never paid attention to the door that hid it. The paint was dingy, and mildew clung close to the pipes. It wasn't a room meant for students, nor teachers.

I cleared my throat, then said nothing.

There was an awkward pause. I thought he was going to badger me about the CAT tests, but he didn't. Instead, he patted my shoulder and said that it was okay. I remember my insides trembling and a rush of tears sliding down my face. I peered at him through the tears, wanting him to drag answers from me, but I wouldn't have told him anyway. Mr. LeBlanc said for me to go back to class when my face was dry, not to rush. He hurried away and left me rooted to the cement, watching the bucket, wondering what I was going to do next. I didn't slip back into class to get my books until the next bell rang. I snatched them and quietly slipped out of the room.

I sat near an open window in my next class, not wanting to look at anyone directly. Daydreaming took over. I turned to the thick windowsill to my left and lazily rested my head on my folded arms to stare at the bustling field of boys playing football. A few pulled their shirts off. Their tanned muscles and sweaty torsos rippled in the hot sun. Two senior boys passed underneath the window. I quickly closed my eyes and feigned sleep.

I overheard bits of their conversation about one of the cheerleaders. I imagined I was a cheerleader, so they'd talk about me. I waited until they were well out earshot before I opened my eyes again. I peeked over my folded arms to make sure they were gone. A pair of hickory-colored eyes looked right back at me.

Vice Principal Burkee.

His forehead became squished when I didn't say anything or even lift my head. I was frozen. He was a tall man, with a head full of silver hair that also poked out of his ears and nose, and unruly brown eyes that seemed to turn flame red when he was angry. They were flame red now. You didn't have to be close to him to know he smelled of Old Spice.

He pointed for me to turn back to my classroom. Slowly, I sat up and pretended to pay attention to my teacher, who was busy at the chalkboard, writing notes I should have been copying. Out of the corner of my eye, I watched Mr. Burkee walk away and scribble something vigorously onto a notepad, his concentration so strong he almost walked into a metal pole.

I didn't know what the scribble was or that it would change my life forever. I glanced back at the field and smiled. The boys were still playing. Still shirtless.

Chapter 10:

Operation Great Escape

—

That evening, things got dangerous for me when I heard heavy footsteps and my door burst open. Dad rushed into my room, grabbing me around the throat with his hands, choking me as I flew back onto my bed. He shouted that I was embarrassing him. Mom stood behind him, bobbing her head in agreement. Mr. Burkee had called Mom and told her that I was purposely failing, that I had failed all the California Achievement Tests with straight zeros across the board, and that I didn't get along with my algebra teacher. Dad unclenched his fingers from around my throat. He waited for me to answer. I explained to him that I didn't know what was going on. He told me to turn around and bend over as he slid his belt off.

I fixed my eyes on Mom—who was avoiding looking directly at me—waiting for her to speak up, to jump in between the leather strap and me, to tell him to leave me alone. To leave her *daughter* alone. I had suspected, even before that evening, that my mother was united in my father's hatred of me, that she thought I was an embarrassment, that I was crazy. Before that evening, I hadn't chosen to believe it, but standing there looking at her not looking at me, in seeing her shame of me, it made my heart turn cold.

I turned and bent over the bed, biting into the comforter as he gave me several lashes across my back. The rushing air let out a hiss each time he swung, but I was determined not to cry. When he stopped, he hurled insults at me. I stood up again and continued to act dumb. "It has to be a computer error," I sputtered. "Why would I fail on purpose?"

My father cocked his head. I didn't have a history of lying, but I was doing it now. Bubba lied all the time, but he wasn't good at it. He didn't know how to confuse our dad. I did. It was called a poker face, and I was wearing it at that moment. For years, Bubba and I played card games. It was all that we had for entertainment. They were innocent games for children, but they taught me how to be unreadable.

Dad was persuaded that I had no reason to fail. He gave me until the next day to sort it out. I looked past him into Mom's face, but she only cast her eyes downward. I understood in that moment, that if I stayed, I would always be alone. Dad stormed off, and Mom followed, without looking back.

I caressed my throat as I realized that it was time to put Operation Great Escape into motion. Tomorrow, I would make my carefully designed move. I was going to run away. After he left the room, I scrambled to get a few of my things in the little time I had. I'd been hoping to make it to summertime before leaving, but at the same time I'd known I wouldn't wait that long. I wasn't going to get stuck living in some godforsaken swamp in a bucket-of-bolts trailer, waiting around to get beaten some more.

I emptied my backpack of old papers and a few books to make room for only the essentials, so I wouldn't look obvious the next morning. I rummaged through my closet and found a compact camouflage military shovel I used for metal detecting, to dig up all the gold I never found. It folded in half and was made for packs, so I tossed it into the bag. Either I'd dig a hole or hit someone with it. I wasn't sure what I needed holes for.

The critical things I needed for survival were my journals Grandma Avis had given me and a good writing pen. I hoped to bump into a publisher on my way to California. I'd watched enough shows and movies to know that the money was out West. I wanted to be rich and famous like them, to have cameras flashing just inches from my face, to have my meals interrupted at restaurants. I decided I would probably audition for a role on my favorite show, *Silver Spoons*, while I was there.

I liked mountains and beaches. California had both, so I would decide which I'd be living on once I got there. I grabbed a bottle of suntan lotion off my dresser and shoved it into the sack with the shovel. The one thing I'd already figured out was a good life—riches and a family—was not going to fall from the sky. If you want something bad enough, you have to grab a shovel and go after it.

I kept my backpack close and could barely sleep. No matter what, I was leaving. I just wanted to find a place where I belonged. I didn't care whether it had grapes, a beach, or just an old rotten tree. I wanted a family, one that would teach me to love and to be a stronger person. Surely, there had to be someone out there who would want a nobody like me. I tore a slip of paper from my journal and wrote that down, then put it in my sole for the next day.

I will find a better life, no matter how far I have to walk. Please help me find it.

It would be my last night in that bedroom. I cried when I thought of never seeing Gabby again, or Bubba, even though we barely talked anymore. We were in the same house but living in two different worlds. Bubba had new friends now, drifting in and out most days, always on the brink of trouble. He smoked cigarettes, chewed tobacco, and stole sacks of crawfish from a local farm (and whatever else he could get his hands on) to resell. He wasn't even out of junior high yet. We now walked different paths for different reasons.

I was still in shock that I was running away to California sooner than I planned, that I was abandoning my family to join the cast of *Silver Spoons*. I figured my parents wouldn't even notice me gone, until late the next evening. By that time, I would be halfway to California.

I remembered when my cousin Josephine ran away from home, one evening, when I was at her house. She had a huge blowout with her mom and screamed that she was leaving. She tossed her clothes in a bag and I trailed along, pleading with her to stay. She made it as far as her friend's house down the road. There was a trampoline out in the backyard. Josephine tossed her bag of clothes on the ground and ran toward it. She screamed at me to jump on, and we bounced and laughed until it felt like our legs and faces would fall off. When darkness came, she grabbed her bag and we trudged back.

When we walked in, my aunt was waiting, belt in hand. Josephine squared herself as she told her mom that she was back for now because she got distracted. My aunt walloped her good, but Josephine cackled like she did when we were on the trampoline. Aunt Sue's face was red, and she had a large vein bulging in her neck as she swung. Josephine's laughter echoed off the walls. I knew I couldn't afford to fail like she had, so I planned on steering clear of all trampolines.

That night, I couldn't sleep. I lay under my armor of quilts and listened to the constant *tick-tick* of the clock that sat on the set of industrial shelves, next to my bed. At 1:00 a.m., I loped out of my bed and removed the lotion from my pack. At 2:00 a.m., I put it back. When 3:00 a.m. rolled around, I decided I didn't need the excess weight and removed it again. After all, I had a secret wad of cash that could buy me bottles of it if I chose. Operation Great Escape was so well-plotted that I was purposefully leaving a stash— over a hundred dollars—that my parents knew about, so they would have no clue that I'd run away from home.

I always had this mental image of how my mom would react when I didn't get off the bus in the afternoon. She'd figure I had just decided to walk home. By the time the sun would start to droop down behind the pines around our neighborhood, Dad would arrive home from work, and I would be no less than ten miles away. Mom would have already searched my room, looking for clues, and found the money in plain sight. They would both tell the police, "She'd never leave her money behind. She must have been kidnapped. There is no other explanation."

That night, my parents would be on the same team. All thoughts of beatings, alcohol, and accusations would be stifled by concerns of my being kidnapped by a total stranger. The police would tell them that I'm probably just a runaway. They see it all of the time. Mom's voice would tremble, but she would say loud and clear, "Tracie is a homebody. She would *never* run away."

Chapter 11:

Winds of Change

—

I fled the next morning, just after sunrise, with my bag containing only the shovel and my journals. It was warm, humid. Mom thought I was going to school. I was going to California. Gravel crunched underneath my feet as I crept down backroads, flinching each time a car rolled past. It would be at least eight hours before anyone knew I was missing, and another five before a police report would be filed. I had a thirteen-hour head start, and I was really, really doing this.

When I reached a four-lane highway, I charged across and pushed my way through a thick tree line to a railroad track. It stretched on a raised bed of gravel, glowing from the rays of the morning sun. On the other side of the track were fields of alfalfa, ablaze with yellow blossoms. I figured I'd walk on the rail bed until dusk and then look for shelter.

Finally, after all I'd been through, everything I had walked for and prayed to God for, I was at the end of nothing and the beginning of everything.

The track was endless, the rust-colored rails a comforting embrace from each side. I didn't know if I'd make it to California or just around the corner—a thousand miles or ten miles. I didn't know what I'd find or when I'd find it, but I would find it. The track ran parallel to the highway but would gradually careen away, slowly putting more distance between civilization and me.

I just want to go forward with my life. Anything has to be better than the life I am living now.

Three hours into my walk I was panting like a dog and tempted to go back. I stared into the distance at a small herd of cows trying to pack themselves into the shade of a thin willow tree. Then I heard the shriek of a loud whistle, followed by a thunderous roar.

I whipped around to see a train in the distance. I didn't want to be seen, so I jumped off the track and tried to camouflage myself in some trees. The *clackity-clack* of the wheels grew louder as it approached. The sound commanded the attention of all other sounds, and I started to feel a small thrum at my feet. As it got closer, I realized that I wanted on that train.

Leaning tighter into the tree, I wiped the sweat from my brow and mentally prepared myself. I hadn't thought about actually riding on a train. Walking was all I knew and all I had expected. I waited for the right moment, until the first car passed by. I didn't trust that the train engineer wouldn't call the police.

The mammoth engine exploded past me, roiling the gravelly dust in its wake as I ran from my hiding spot. As I drew close to the train, I was hit by a tidal wave of wind, my hair whipped furiously, and I stopped to rethink my plan. I stood in awe of the train's massiveness as it ripped right through the air. That train was probably going to California, to the beaches, to the money, and all the grapes I could eat.

I took off running again, looking for some part to grab hold of. There weren't many boxcars. Most looked like the tank cars that were parked along the track in El Dorado, and the pungent smell coming off them began to overwhelm me. I briefly stopped to catch my breath, looking for the right car to grab. A few red ones covered with graffiti were coming up. After a quick breather, I started running again.

I stumbled on the incline of rocks and struggled to keep my balance. More than anything ever, I wanted to be on this train. As the first red car got close, I started gaining momentum and reached out to grab a bar on the lower corner. Just as my fingers touched the bar, my left shoe caught the edge of a railroad tie. I flew hard onto the gravel, my face hitting another tie that was sticking out. I rolled down the embankment and lay crumpled, my body vibrating from the ground beneath me, as my hope shot past me in a blaze of glorious thunder.

I put my hands over my ears as the train roared past, the wind still relentless. I looked up and watched the train get smaller and heard the shriek of the whistle fade into the distance, swallowed by the horizon I'd been walking toward for hours. Blood was flowing out of my nose, so I rolled over and pinched my nostrils together, thinking about what I had just done.

I was supposed to be in school, staring at shirtless, sweaty boys on the football field, not running alongside trains trying to jump into moving boxcars like a hobo. I'd already talked to three cows, and the day wasn't over. Yes, the people of my little town would really have something to gossip about if they knew where I was. But they didn't have to live with my dad.

For the first time in my life, I just wanted to catch a train. Specifically, that train. I hoisted myself up and stepped back onto the track, wiping away the limestone dust caked on my clothing. Another train would come along, maybe a better one with more boxcars. Surely, this wouldn't be the only one. I looked down to see that my shoe was torn.

A few more hours into my walk, I discovered a snakeskin on the other side of the rail. I held it up as the light breeze shifted it. I thought about keeping it, stuffing it in my pack with the shovel, but then realized that I didn't need an old snakeskin. Even the snake didn't want it. I held it up and let it flutter away in the wind.

As I walked, I felt just like that snake did. I was slowly shedding the old me. After only a few hours, I already felt older, wiser, and full of promise. This is what freedom does to a person. It rebirths them. When I emerged from the other side of this track, I would be transformed. This was who I was going to be.

But each time I lost my footing, my left sole tore a little more, and I felt a little less excited. Being exposed to direct sun was wearing me down. As dehydration started setting in, I had trouble keeping a good pace. My seven years of dreaming had not involved thirst, hunger, or exhaustion. The visions in my head always involved comforts I hadn't had before. There was no comfort here.

I pulled my shoes off and fished out some of the papers inside, reading each one out loud to the rails. When I finished, I refolded them and carefully tucked them back in. I stood and looked back in the direction I had come from, and then I looked in the direction I was heading. It wasn't too late to go back. But I decided there was nothing to go back to.

A BUZZARD WITH SOOTY black plumage ogled me as it stood over the furry carcass of a large dog, or small cow, that probably got hit by a train. I didn't know if buzzards attacked living things, so I passed with caution. It sidestepped and flapped its wings at me, daring me to enter its space. The thought occurred to me that maybe I looked like roadkill. I certainly felt like it.

Finally, after hours of walking, a store sprang into sight. It was a great relief to walk into air conditioning, and I quickly went to the back to drink from the fountain and clean up. The water was so refreshing.

After I left the store, I had to walk a few miles before I finally saw some oak trees over a side road, creating a dark shelter in the heavy brush underneath their canopies. I decided this would be a good place for me to make camp for the night. As I headed toward the forest, I noticed a truck passing. I held the straps of my pack tightly and scurried faster. The truck stopped and shifted in reverse, watching me turn down the side road. I noticed two men inside the truck. Their eyes followed me as I turned onto a worn path, leading into the trees.

A thin bayou meandered through the center of the wooded area. It was muddy and thick, so I couldn't tell how deep it was. Trees stood at attention, their dark shadows mingling with the contrasting blues and purples of irises dotted along the edge.

I felt safest camping by the bayou, farther from the road. Although I knew I was still close to town, I was most afraid of bears, but I had the compact shovel in my backpack for a weapon. For the first time in my life, I was truly alone. My eyes grew big, darting from sound to sound, hoping serial killers weren't living among the trees. Nothing could have prepared me for this. My heart was pounding as the hushed blackness started to smother me.

I stood in the forest that was slowly growing dark, preparing myself to be brave. The trees were crammed close together and leaned toward a tiny clearing. I decided to settle there and walked gently, so as not to draw the forest's attention.

Slivers of light showed through the trees, just enough for me to write by. I swatted at mosquitoes as crickets chirped in the background and small animals rustled in the leaves. My pen scratched only one line as the wind howled through the trees and coyotes yipped in the distance. *The world is less scary now.*

I heard a rustling and glanced up to the path I had just walked. One of the thick, black branches moved. Then it started to coil. My breath hushed.

I'd lived in southern Louisiana long enough to know what a water moccasin looked like. It looked like a branch. *That* branch. I wanted to run, but quietly I slipped my pack over my shoulder. The snake threatened me with its wide-open cotton mouth. I backed up, never taking my eyes off it, until I was far enough away. My options were limited. Once I was at a safe distance, I scrambled through the moss and trees. It occurred to me that I could have used my shovel to chop the snake's head off.

I found another small clearing and tree to lean against. After an hour, I got used to sitting still. I was comforted by the soft glow of the moonlight. The air gently came alive with sounds, but not human noises, and for that I was glad. There was a little more clarity in the forest on my own. I tensed with every sound, listened deeper, heard more. If I didn't know the source of a sound, I tried not to panic, focusing instead on succeeding in my journey.

A twig snapped, a loud and crisp sound from a heavy weight, like a bear or Bigfoot. Could there really be bears out here? I held my breath, lest bears could smell breath. My pack was nearly empty. The only food I had to offer was me, and I wasn't offering. Another twig cracked, this time louder. A voice seared the darkness, "Be quiet, she'll hear us."

Then: "Did you bring the rope?"

I fled.

I knew that if I ran toward the road, I would land straight into the speaker's arms. My only option was to scramble toward the snake.

I rushed through the darkness in the direction of the snake. I couldn't see well, but as I grew closer to where it was, I gambled and took a sharp right, hoping it was still curled in the same spot as before, and then I veered in the direction of the bayou.

Twigs snapped violently behind me. The men were gaining on me. The bayou was lit by the moon. I wasn't sure if I could make it across. One of the men screamed. The other man shouted, "Snake!" I didn't look back. I arched my body and leapt.

My sneakers landed hard on the other side. I clambered up a small embankment.

Then I ran.

I pushed my way through dense brush a few hundred feet. In the distance, a bright light beamed. There was another back road where a few homes were scattered. I made out the outline of a shed and once I reached it, collapsed in the dirt. After a couple minutes of gasping, a dog began to bark. I decided to move on and find shelter.

I walked along the edge of the road at first, fearful someone could see me. After about twenty minutes, there were few houses, fewer cars. I was enveloped by darkness—a pitch-black—the kind that cloaks the hinterlands of civilization, where artificial light is almost nonexistent, where the moonlight tumbles undisputed from the sky. I ambled over to the center of the road, keeping a vigilant eye out for headlights.

Sometimes, I did a little dance on the asphalt to break the monotony of my lonely walk. I imagined I was a famous ballerina and practiced my stance. Then I pretended to slow dance with someone. I could do anything I wanted to, so I danced in a happy stupor, just because I could. My dance wasn't perfect, and I didn't care. As the day's heat withered away, I waltzed the rest of the way down the long road, the papers in my shoes dancing with me.

AS I MADE MY way into town there were two women and a man trawling along the edge of a street corner. I slipped down a side road where some apartment buildings were and wandered between them until I saw a small, empty laundromat that belonged to the complex. I went in and noticed that it could lock from the inside. I closed the door, locked it, and turned down the lights. This would be perfect shelter for the night. I slipped into a large empty basket that sat under a table, covering up with an old shirt someone had left behind.

All throughout the night, headlight beams crept up and down the walls, as if they were searching for me, just barely missing me. As the hours passed, I got used to the dim city noises, the dull hum of a streetlight outside. In the hushed moments, I thought about the snake and the men. I evaded all of them, but they found each other in the darkness. The entire day had felt like a movie, each frame more intense than the last.

And here I was at the end, in a laundry basket.

THE NEXT MORNING, the hum of the streetlight was gone and replaced by a cacophony of noises. Doors slamming, cars honking, life stirring. The events from the evening before had frightened me pretty good. I began to realize that there were men as bad as, or worse, than my dad. I had to keep moving, so I headed toward a local high school that was around the bend. It was secluded enough that I could sit and regroup without drawing any attention. It was a Saturday, so there should've been only a few people there, if any. When I made the corner, I noticed quite a few cars. Since school was ending in a few months, teachers were preparing for senior graduation.

I remembered that Mr. LeBlanc's wife worked at this school. I slipped inside. A teacher stopped and asked if she could help me with anything. Without giving it any thought, I asked if Ms. LeBlanc was in. I was tired, thirsty, and hungry. I needed to trust someone. "Yes," the lady replied. "I saw her just a few minutes ago. I'll go get her for you."

A few minutes later, a woman with dark wavy hair and black glasses that dangled on a chain around her neck approached me with a giant smile on her face. "Someone said you wanted to speak with me?"

"Well, you don't know me, but my name is Tracie—"

She grabbed me by the shoulder and ushered me into a room. "Oh, yes, I do know who you are. My husband has talked about you all year. He's been worried sick about you. He called me this morning and said the police were at the school, looking for you. He said you wouldn't open up to him, but darling," she said as she put her hand in mine, "I hope you will open up to me."

There was something about her that made me blurt out everything that I'd been through. I chronicled my childhood, careful not to leave out a thing. I told her how Dad had lined our windows with trash bags to block out the world, the beatings of my mother and brother, and the sleepless nights. I told her about the sexual abuse that started when I was seven, how he would threaten me with a gun, and I even told her about Lena. When I was done, I asked if she would help me.

"I figured it was something along those lines. Yes, I will help you."

"Please don't let me go back there."

"You won't, trust me."

Ms. LeBlanc made some phone calls, and a squad car showed up to take me to the police station. I didn't want to leave Ms. LeBlanc, but she told me not to worry. After I told my story again at the station, a social worker named Marla ambled in and explained that she was bringing me to a foster home. It was only a two-week placement, and then I would be transferred someplace else. I told her that I didn't know what a foster home was, and she explained that I would live with a temporary family, until the situation with my family was resolved. She went on to tell me that their names were Kate and James, and their two daughters were eight- and five-years-old. The other two children in their home were foster children—a brother and sister. I was happy to hear that there would be children there but still nervous. *What kind of people are they? Will they be nice to me? Will I be happy?* I wasn't thrilled about the idea of living with complete strangers. If something went wrong, I'd be right back at square one.

The ride was long. The trees along the highway swayed, as the sun cast brilliant rays in the direction we were headed. I was nervous and regretted not packing one of the small iron horses that Grandma Avis had given me, just to hold in the palm of my hand for comfort. I thought about the last few years of my life and recalled the story of Wind Horse. Like the distant beat of a drum, our path beckons. The sound gets heavier, quaking the ground underneath us, shaking the earth. Calling. The brave venture out. Decisions must be made. Some press forward. And then the winds of change finally blow.

PART TWO

Chapter 12:

Copious Power

—

As soon as we pulled up, a cheerful woman with long blond hair came rushing out the house to greet us. Her name was Kate, and she said they'd been anxiously awaiting my arrival. I had never felt so welcome before. She put her arms around my shoulders and led me inside. I felt out of place wearing my safari shirt and clung awkwardly to my shovel. Marla had Kate sign some paperwork, then left.

The house was bustling with people. Two men were installing a counter table of sorts. It extended out of the kitchen like a long, curved table, but they hadn't put the Formica top on just yet, so it was just a rounded piece of bare wood. It had dozens of names and messages scrawled on it. I nervously stared at it.

My foster dad's name was James. He had a bushy beard and short hair. The other man, who was helping to install the counter, was his friend. I was introduced to the other children as well: Lisa, the oldest; her younger sister Julie; the two small foster children, Michael, and Jen. Someone put a pen in my hand and told me to scrawl my name on the wood, like everyone else had done.

They want me to put my name with theirs.

Writing my name and having it sealed up with the laminate, like a promise, softened the moment. It seemed to me that it was a sign from God, affirmation of *his* divine assurance that despite my hardships, beyond a doubt, God would engineer a train and rail me to my next destination.

Kate surveyed me with one eyebrow raised, her eyes resting on my boy's khaki shirt with flap pockets. I looked like a poacher. She uncurled my fingers from the shovel and handed it to James.

"We are going shopping," she said.

Moments later, we climbed into a two-tone brown van, and together we lurched onto the highway. As she drove, I studied her profile. She had golden curls that tumbled down her back and creamy skin, reflecting off amber light shining through the windows. I stared optimistically at Kate.

Kate helped me to match colors with skirts, blouses, jeans, and tops. She seemed to be very good at it, and I liked the look and feel of the clothing on me. In the dressing room, I found myself staring in the mirror, wondering how I went from walking on a railroad track to shopping for clothes—nicer clothes than I had ever had before.

It felt odd to be shopping without Bubba. We'd always been together, and now we weren't. My mom had bought me matching boy boots once while shopping with him, and I cried so hard that she brought them back and let me buy some plastic loafers instead. I was safe now, shopping, but Bubba was left behind. I tried not to think of him as I ran my fingers across a striped pink-and-white shirt Kate had picked out. I looked up at her smiling face, teeth glistening. I liked it and so did she.

My first week in foster care flew by in a rush of meetings and registering for a new school, punctuated by morning and evening church services. My other minutes were filled with Kate chauffeuring me from one place to another. A meeting was scheduled for me to meet my parents and decide my fate. After seven years of walking for a better life, I was now being asked to decide my future.

The next Sunday, my parents showed up at the church that I now attended. For the last few years, I had walked a block every Sunday to attend a small church by myself. Now, here they were, attending a church more than thirty miles from where they lived, sitting in the back row. I glanced in their direction. Dad's eyes were coldly staring at me.

Dad had his delivery route changed. He began navigating his big brown truck past our house every day. One evening, I went outside in the front yard to read a book. I could not remember a section of time where I could stretch out and relax, without listening to Dad accuse or beat someone. I had only read a few pages when I heard the familiar revving of a bubble truck. I glanced up to see Dad, piloting it past our house, blades of grass bending awkwardly as it swooshed past. He waved. A few minutes later, he passed by again, his eyes fixed on me. I stood up and went inside. I trudged down the hall to my bedroom. He was sending me a message through the roar of the truck: *I'll always find you.*

James had a buoyant and devout wit about him and thrived on daily inspirations from his Bible. Each evening he sat under a lamplight, reading different scriptures. If he saw me, he'd pat the sofa and invite me to join in on the reading. He would select a passage from the Bible and read it aloud, while I sat next to him, breathing in the woodsy scent of his cologne as I listened. Heaven was dangled in front of me, glowing gold with beautiful streams and valleys.

He told me the story of David and Goliath. I'd heard the story before, but the way James told it made me feel as if I were crouched on a ridge outside Israel, surrounded by fields of blazing wheat and valleys. I felt connected. I imagined David, about the same age as me, walking alone down a valley to do single combat with a hulking giant of a man who is glittering with armor. I pictured David, armorless, whirling a stone. Goliath's laughter echoes through the hills, drowned by the cackles of his comrades. Moments later, the behemoth man's body folds to the ground, unconscious.

"Then, David slayed the giant," James said.

I whispered, "What about Goliath's army?"

There was a drawn-out pause.

"They left," he said.

A week later, I had my first visit with my parents; they brought with them my grandmother Avis and Aunt Carol. Mom was wearing a new print dress, and her eyes shimmered like a movie star. Dad was dressed in button-up shirt and dress slacks. Kate stayed in the lobby while the social worker led everyone into a small room with a window. They showered me with gifts, expensive clothes, and a watch. When the visit was over, the worker led us back to the lobby. Once there, Dad turned toward me and said that I would go live in northern Louisiana with Grandma and Aunt Carol. I tilted my head. I didn't understand. He cleared his throat and repeated it again. I would go live with my grandmother, until this was resolved.

I remembered the times my mother had gone to their house. I imagined myself skidding down long stretches of highway, all the way to Grandma's little house in West Monroe. I pictured myself sharing a room with my two younger cousins. I also pictured my dad showing up days later to fetch me, whispering in my ear he had a loaded shotgun in his truck.

I was forging my own path, and my family needed to realize that. There was a time in my life when I wouldn't have stood up to anyone in my family. I would have dipped my head and, with shoulders slumped, blindly followed along. But I wasn't the same person I had been two weeks before.

Every inch of ground I had walked, every mile I had ran, seven years of hoping and prayer had granted me this one license: to narrate my own life without Dad's voice in it. I had Kate and James, and I was starting to feel that they were my family, that they would always be there for me. After all, my name was under the Formica countertop, right along with theirs. Even though I was only a temporary placement in their home, I wanted to believe that everyone in that house was my family, and we would be together forever.

Dad and I were at a deadlock. I took a deep breath and stared him down. There was an instant hush, so intense, the room felt shattered by it. No breaths were taken, no feet shuffled. Everyone staring at me thought I was incredibly weak, but what they didn't understand was this: the fifteen-year-old girl standing nervously before them had a rock to sling.

"I'm not going," I said.

Mom's face sank. Clamping a frown, Dad leaned forward to whisper something in my ear. I took a step back and the whisper stuck in his throat. His eyes narrowed; his face hardened like steel. Two minutes later, they all filed out of the building.

Without me.

JAMES CONTINUED TO READ to me in the evenings and tell me different stories from the Bible. When the reading was over, he would hug me and tell me that he loved me. Each time he did this, I sat in a paralytic unease, unable to respond. This made me believe that I could never be as pious as James, because I had nothing to give. All my belief was tucked secretly in my shoes, and I'd never have the courage to share it, never have the courage to love. I shrank back from their hugs and words of love, and eventually, it became clear to me that maybe I had miscalculated the fluid reality of being in the outside world. Maybe my dad's world was the only one I could ever be a part of.

Slowly, I felt myself coming to life, but I knew it was not fast enough.

I imagined myself straddling the rocky vent of a volcano, magma bubbling and boiling beneath me. James and Kate's love was that magma. I teetered nervously on the edge, afraid of falling in, terrified of getting burned. I was starved for love, but much like someone who had walked through a desert and hadn't eaten or drunk for a long time, too much of it at once made me want to vomit.

James never yelled at me. His voice was soft and kind. He tried to make me laugh, but I was not used to kindness. It was lobbed at me like a baseball, and I didn't know how to catch it. I was used to anger and screaming. I didn't know how to give or receive anything good. I had always been in control of my dad, outsmarted him. Here, I had no reason to be smarter than James, nor the desire. I still found myself struggling to sleep at night—but not because of James. Dad still haunted me in my dreams. His face materialized when I stared into the dark and his warm whiskey breath wafted throughout my room. He wouldn't let me go.

One afternoon, Kate and James came to me and said that they liked me so much I didn't have to leave. I could live with them permanently if I liked. They wrapped their arms around me. I told them I would love to stay and then felt so overwhelmed I disappeared into my room.

My body felt animated with a rush of copious power. I no longer felt suspended between two worlds: the one I had always lived and the one I always wanted. I had just been given permission to stay and be part of a loving family, for exactly what I had spent seven years walking. I did a mental calculation. It had taken over 2,500 days of walking and believing. I wanted to run back to the little town I had come from, scale the tallest building, and from the top, holler as loud as I could across the streets and bayou. *Do you see who I am? I am somebody! My wishes get granted!*

MY PARENTS HAD TO SAVE FACE with the neighbors, so they visited them and explained that I had concocted this awful story about my father. I imagined Dad talking about my grades in school, how I was afraid of punishment. Armed with lies, I ran away from home. I pictured my mother's head bobbing in agreement. Perhaps Mom—even though she was a reserved, peaceful woman—was caught up in Dad's fictional narrative of our lives. Maybe she was starting to believe the reality he carved up for those who were on the outside. Or maybe she wanted to believe it.

Serene moments of normalcy crept into my life in the little things that Kate did for me. Showing me how to apply mascara, styling my hair, telling me how nice I looked in a dress. I treasured my time with her, basking in the attention she floated my way. One day, she took me to a hair stylist and told them to cut off my long lion mane and highlight it. I watched as the stylist snipped thick stalks of my hair off and let it drop to the floor. Kate then told me that she loved the new me.

The new me.

My hair didn't poof on the sides anymore. My father had never allowed me to cut my hair, and after all the years of bullying that I'd endured for it, I only had to cut it short for it to look nice. I watched as the stylist took a corn broom, swept the remnants of my mane into a pan, and emptied it into the garbage.

I became attached to the four children in my foster home. I played board games with them and took them outside when the weather was nice. Jen, the youngest, wore granny glasses that had an elastic band on them to keep them from falling off her face. Some evenings, I read books to the children with Jen in my lap. Michael, the only boy, shadowed me. Lisa was eight but highly intelligent, with a quick, sarcastic wit about her. Julie was five years old, petite, and particular about everything she wore and ate. Slowly, I blended in with this family and earned the right to have my name scrawled in pen under the Formica countertop.

Late one night, after I had fallen asleep, Jen decided to climb into bed with me, something she'd never done before. Before I realized what was going on, she vomited on me. I didn't want to wake Kate, so I cleaned it up myself, wrapped Jen tightly in a blanket, and removed the sheets from the bed. I didn't want to put Jen back in her bed while she was sick, so I held her in the rocking chair in the living room. The rest of the night I kissed her forehead and whispered in her ear that I'd always be there for her.

I WAS MESMARISED BY KATE, her toughness, how she could command a room just by entering it. When she was angry her eyes seared right into you, leaving you smoldering with guilt, even if you weren't the one who'd crossed her. I gawked at her tenacity like she was superhero. On a warm July evening, as all the children were helping me, Kate snuck a water hose in and sprayed us with it. We all ran for cover as Lisa, without missing a beat, filled a glass of water and lobbed it toward Kate. Somehow, eggs got involved next. We all laughed, but I panicked at the sight of the kitchen. Kate said not to worry, that a kitchen could be dried and cleaned up, and eggs were only $0.69 a dozen, but laughter and memories—much like words—were what stayed forever with us, and there was no price that could be put on that.

It was a Friday night. I was in my room with Karen, a daughter of some friends who were over visiting Kate and James. They were the

Franklins. Mr. Franklin was a tall man with glasses, a protruding belly, and a little pat of baldness that he covered over with a path of combed-over hair. His wife wore thicker glasses, and her voice was as sweet as molasses.

Karen had a quiet demeanor and dark hair that tumbled down her back like black silk. I mentioned to her that I needed to do something to set myself apart, to show Kate that I was trying to socialize and improve myself. She tilted her head at me. "You could help us with our puppet show next week." The Franklins had a children's ministry, and they would travel to different churches doing puppet shows, usually in the evenings. We raced to her parents to ask permission, then to Kate and James. Everyone agreed. I would travel with the Franklins. That night, I packed a few clothes and left with them to stay in their camper, which was stacked with black cases and books filled with scripts. I stayed with them in the camper for several days, while they were readying for the trip.

Mr. Franklin opened case after case of puppets and introduced me to them all. On Friday morning, almost a week later, we traveled to a church and dragged the cases of puppets out the camper. A group of four teenaged boys from the youth group were waiting for us. Like me, they were to be trained to perform with the puppets. The other teenagers and I set up the puppet stage, attaching small rods and curtains. We had to rework it a few times to get it just right. Finally, Mr. Franklin came over and surveyed the stage. "It is ready."

I was handed a puppet called Fred and slipped it on like a glove. I stared optimistically at the puppet sleeved on my arm. Surely, I could do this. I practiced and practiced, moving just the bottom jaw of Fred. The six of us shuffled around behind the stage, exchanging puppets, and practicing lines, which for some reason I kept forgetting.

Mr. Franklin was very serious about the success of his shows; I wasn't sure if I was up to the challenge. When I missed a line, he snapped at me. I looked at him as he adjusted his wire-rimmed glasses and told him I was sorry. He muttered something inaudible as I turned back to the puppet and tried to remember the line. I cast my eyes downward when the words didn't come to me. Mr. Franklin called for a break, and everyone set down their puppets and moved to the kitchen. Alone, behind the puppet stage, I raked my eyes across the empty cases and abandoned puppets. I sat quietly, thinking about how I couldn't remember any words. In a sea of frowning puppets, I felt like a failure.

After the break, Mr. Franklin began talking about the crowd that was expected for the show. It would probably be a full house. He told us to fetch more chairs, so Karen and I followed some of the boys to a back room and loaded our arms with all the extra folding chairs we could carry. I lined them tightly along the back wall, imagining that evening when, as the seats filled with dozens of strangers, I'd have to give a flawless performance.

I had hoped that the puppet show would be the perfect opportunity for me to shine in front of Kate and James. In all fairness, I should have nailed it. It just wasn't possible. I had only been with Kate and James for two months, and this new reality was not yet mine to take. I knew I should try to devote myself to being the person Kate wanted me to be. But I was too afraid of failing, not just Kate, but also myself. When crowds of people thronged through the door, I became anxious. My head started to thrum, and the room spun. I was going to pass out with my arm jammed halfway up the rear end of a puppet. With every minute, I became more terrified of disappointing Kate, James, God, and the crowd that was filing into the sanctuary.

I peeked from behind the curtain. The room was writhing with people, many more than I expected. I remember that night clearly, the moment when I saw Kate and James walk through the sanctuary door and realized how much I had missed them. I had a full-on panic attack. The puppet became a fuzzy blur. My fear took control.

I held my breath and counted to ten, then walked over to Mr. Franklin and told him I didn't think I could do it. His face sank. He barked that I'd committed to the puppet show, that I'd be letting down all the children. And God. "God," he repeated. Then his eyes softened as if he knew that was a harsh statement and just stared at the wall behind me as he continued droning on about how I was letting everyone down. I stood quietly, knowing the puppet show could continue without me. It always had before. The lights from above reflected off his glasses like tiny lasers. He stood motionless, but for the trembling of his hands. "Thanks for the week," I said and walked past the stage into the audience, in search of Kate and James. They were shocked that I didn't want to perform, but James told me not to worry about it. The show was wonderful, and I wished I'd had the courage to be a part of it. The Franklins never came around again, and I never questioned why.

Decades later, I saw a puppet show at a church with my foster children and remembered the Franklins. It made me realize how weak I was as a teenager, so long ago. Maybe I wasn't as strong as I thought I'd been.

———

I FIRST MET LINDSEY in the lunchroom at school. We sat near each other. She had three earrings in one ear and two in the other. Her hair seemed to be dyed darker than whatever it was naturally. She told me she was in foster care. I reluctantly told her that I was too. It felt shameful to confess that. It made me think of how my parents had failed as parents, and I had failed as their child, so I kept it a secret from the world. Lindsey had been in five foster homes in two years, not including a group home.

My eyebrows raised in shock at this. "I've only been in one, but it will probably be my only one," I said.

She let out a chilled laugh and rolled her eyes. "You are such a greenie."

"A what?"

"You're green, and I can tell you're trusting. Probably naïve too."

I nodded. I tended to trust everyone, and I was very naïve. Someone had once told me that the reason I was so pale was because I had moon burn, and for years after that I had tried to stay in after dark and hide myself from the light of the moon.

"They'll always be your first, but not your last," she said. "Just like a boyfriend, they suck. They're always trying to get the best foster kids they can, like trading up. Someone was there before you and someone will be there after you. When the going gets tough, they wave goodbye and send you on your way."

My greenness had been apparent to Lindsey, and as I gnawed on the remnants of a carrot, I realized I must have looked like such a fool. To believe that I could waltz right into normalcy, blending in with a family like I'd always been a part of it, was ridiculous. I wanted to stay green, to be young and innocent forever, to believe that the dreams that had come true for me would always stay so. They must stay so. Years of walking had made me believe that this was my right.

"Oh no, not these people," I finally said. "We get along fine. No problems, really."

"I know you want to believe that, and I've also thought that about the best people, but you're just part of a production line. I've been shipped out so many times, I don't even care anymore. Besides, in two more years, I'll age out anyway."

"Age out?"

"You really don't know much about foster care, do you? Once you reach eighteen, the state stops paying, the check stops coming, and they kick you out onto the street. It's called aging out of the system," she said with a slight eye roll. The bell rang. "Well, I gotta go. Good luck. See you around, Greenie." We had lunch for a few days after that, but then one day she was gone. I figured she must have been shipped out.

After living with Kate and James for months, I knew I'd made the right decision to run away. Life was amazing. I believed my problems had been left behind, like an abandoned building. I didn't know it at the time, but they were about to get worse.

Lindsey had jinxed me; the universe abruptly changed gears. Within a week, Kate told me that she and James were sending Michael and Jen to another foster home because I had made her realize that teens were less stress on her. A shivering sensation pulsed through my body. I felt light-headed and needed to lie down. Without saying much, I lumbered down the hall to my room where I collapsed on my bed. They were trading up with two people I had grown to love and care about. Anger and resentment seared my thoughts. Deep down, I realized that it was difficult for Kate to have four small children. But I was still struggling not to see my own brother and sister—and now, these were being shipped out. Because of me. What if Jen got sick again? What if she had no one to go to? Who was she going to throw up on? It was a lot for me to take in. I'd become too attached.

In the following days, I took long bike rides, pedaling endlessly to the rhythm of the quiet around me, but clobbering myself in the hinterlands of my mind with resounding slaps of self-accusation. I was only a few months into foster care but felt a great shift in my selfdom. I pedaled around the giant subdivision, passing rows of neatly laid-out homes. Riding had always been my quiet retreat—to think, pray, plan. Had I one-upped the kids so much that I knocked them out the picture completely? What had I done? How could I fix this? I had to do something. I had to save them. So, I fought with myself about the situation. Tossed and turned at night. Pedaled during the day. I decided that it was best for Kate, but I still resented her for it.

When a new family was found for them, I still had no solution. The last night that they stayed with us, Michael tiptoed into my room and asked if he could sleep with me. I said yes, even though he was supposed to stay in his own room. This was probably the worst thing he could have done.

Holding him through the night made his leaving more real. Occasionally, I heard him sob, his hand clinging tightly to mine. I wanted to go with them, just to make sure they were being looked after. I felt obligated. Because I had kept such a keen eye on Gabby when she was younger, I felt that I was in charge of kids, like it was my responsibility to keep all children in the world safe from creatures of the night.

We packed up the kids the next morning and met a couple at a fast-food restaurant to transfer them. Their names were April and Raymond. April seemed friendly and greeted the children warmly. They lived in the country with a few animals, mostly chickens, and lots of room for the children to play. They had five children of their own. Both children warmed up quickly to April and Raymond, and when they left in a giant blue van, Michael waved energetically through the window.

As the days passed, I felt undeserving, somehow deeply at fault for the children no longer being there. The guilt I felt became all-consuming. Each day, something breathed this sensation into me, and I felt everyone around me but my foster parents could sense that it was my fault. I would quickly learn that in the world of foster care, when one child left, another would always materialize as a replacement.

One day a teenage girl appeared in the doorway. Her name was Amy. She and I were four weeks apart in age. Permed hair flowed down her shoulders and mascara accentuated her deep blue eyes.

The first thing Amy did was apologize for being so beautiful. It is extremely difficult to weed people out, she declared. Looking me up and down she said, "Don't worry; we'll fix this with a makeover."

As she had with me, Kate decided right away that Amy needed to go shopping. She ordained that Amy could skip school and they would go to the mall the next day. I wanted to come too, but Kate said that I had to go to school. I reminded her that I'd done all my homework and didn't have any tests, but she just waved her hand and told me no.

They came back that afternoon with bags and bags of clothing. Amy ran to the bedroom with a bag and came back in minutes with new clothes on. I settled on the couch and edged closer to Kate, hoping she would ask me about my day, but her hands were clasped together, and her head was busy bobbing up and down in approval of Amy, who was modeling the holy grail of jeans—Guess brand.

I lumbered my way through the kitchen and out a side door where I perched on a wooden swing. Moments later, Amy followed and sat down beside me. She was still wearing her new jeans and pulled a pack of cigarettes out of a pocket. After she had lit one and puffed into the air, I asked if Kate knew that she smoked.

"Sure," she said, blowing smoke in my direction. "Kate said she's not going to try to change me." She paused. "She is strict though. Maybe I can change that about her."

"I doubt it," I replied.

"Maybe you too."

"I seriously doubt that."

Amy smiled out of the corner of her mouth and blew smoke again. "We'll see."

CHAPTER 13:

SISTERS

There was a side of Amy that made me like her, despite everything she said about me. She could be a lot of fun, and sometimes we'd horse around and cackle until it felt like our guts were about to split wide open. She'd prance around the room in nothing more than a brassiere and underwear, imitating different people.

"Don't drink or smoke, or you'll go straight to hell, I tell you! Directly to the fire and brimstone." Then she'd slam her fist down on a desk like it was a podium and shout, "That goes for all you, heathens." I asked her who she was imitating, and she said just about anyone in this overly religious hick town.

"Even me?" I asked.

"Especially you," she said. I fell on the floor, laughing until my ribs hurt, while she sat on the bed, half naked, pretending to be me reading the Bible.

"I'd have more clothes on than that," I said, but she just replied that she didn't have any old lady clothes handy to fulfill the part of being me.

She taught me how to perfect the art of wearing makeup and how to use the mascara wand to make my lashes curl inward and appear longer and fuller. Occasionally, I stabbed myself in the eye and walked around with a giant black dot on the white of my eye. She showed me how to stretch my hair out with the curling iron and how to dab just the right amount of base on my face, before delicately applying a neutral power to soften the look.

Kate arranged for Amy and me to be in all the same classes. This infuriated Amy. She accused me of being Kate's spy. Besides that, she pointed out, I wasn't cool enough to be around her. She didn't like my taste in clothing, nor the fact that I read an unusual number of books. No one wants to be around a nerd, she told me.

"Don't tell people we are sisters, because we *aren't*." She emphasized the last word, so that there would be no misunderstanding on my part that we were not, and never would be, sisters.

I told her I understood. It didn't bother me, at first, that we were in all the same classes together, but Amy told me that she didn't want to see me twenty-four hours a day. After a few weeks of hearing her rant about it, I decided I didn't want to see her that much either.

I AWOKE, DOUBLED OVER, with the breath knocked out of me. The room was pitch-black. I'd gone to bed hours earlier. I heard shallow breathing on my side.

"Chase me," Amy said.

I pulled the breath back in my chest that was forced out.

"Leave me alone," I moaned.

I felt fingers on my scalp; I was dragged out of bed by my hair. I hit the floor. Amy jumped on top of me, pinning me down, hammering me in the shoulder with her fist. I bit my bottom lip. I didn't want to wake Kate and James.

"This place is boring," she whispered. "Chase me."

I kicked her off; she cackled, then charged out the door. I jerked to my feet. The house was deafeningly silent. I crept into the living room, searching for her in the dark with my hands, wincing when two metal objects clanged. Something swung into my head, and I fell forward. Amy started pounding me with it. I could tell she was swinging the giant stuffed rabbit she slept with. After a few moments of this, I was able to wrestle the rabbit away from her.

"That was fun," she laughed.

I didn't reply. I chucked the rabbit aside and walked past her, into our room. She followed; I yanked my pillow and a blanket off the bed we shared.

"I'm just trying to turn you into a fun person," she said.

I trudged in the living room and tossed my pillow on the couch, where I dropped my body onto it.

When we got home from school the next day, I scratched some words on a slip of paper—*I want to be happy again*—and slipped it in my sole. I yanked my bike off the back patio and rode until dusk. I began riding every day, trying to convince myself that maybe I'd had a good life before foster care. I tried to jam my mind with false memories, conjuring a loving family and loyal friends, but those memories wouldn't register. My mind sent them straight to a slush pile. The memories I was left with looked like they came straight out of a war zone.

IT WAS A THURSDAY evening, late. Amy and I were in the kitchen, the sink bubbling with suds, a stack of dishes waiting to be washed. It was our last chore of the day. Every evening we did laundry and cleaned the kitchen. After that, we were free to do as we pleased. The phone rang. Amy and I both raced for it. I grabbed the receiver and put it to my ear. It was Bubba. He'd run away and spent all of his saved-up yard maintenance money—almost a hundred dollars—on a taxi to our town.

Bubba made me promise that I would help him, that I wouldn't let him get sent back home. I promised that he wasn't going back. Kate said that Bubba could sleep in a spare bed for the night, but he had to meet with Social Services the next day, while I was at school. Bubba asked if he could stay with me at Kate and James's place. "Do you think they'll let me?" he asked. He focused on my face, his eyes glossy, waiting for my reply. I already knew he couldn't. There weren't enough bedrooms in the home. Foster care would require him his own room. But he deserved help, and an answer. I pondered what I should say, foraged my mind for words that would give him hope. After a few moments, I still had nothing. Finally, I said, "Kate will take care of everything. Don't worry."

I begged her to let me stay home from school, but she said no, that she would take care of everything. I slipped into the room where Bubba would be sleeping to tell him that everything would be all right, Kate would fix this. We hugged. He was scared. The next day I came home from school and looked around for him. Kate called me in her room. She took my hand and said that Social Services had brought him back home; they'd found no evidence of abuse against Bubba and that he was just a runaway. I couldn't believe what I was hearing. I felt guilty to be encircled by a loving family, while he had been hastily shipped back.

My brother haunted my dreams that night. I hadn't even been able to tell him bye. I wished the social worker would have allowed me to speak up for him. Bubba and I were both terrified of our dad, but he was more so. Dad hit Bubba harder, gave him less slack. Still, he would not have snitched on Dad with quite the willingness I had. I wondered why my brother and sister hadn't also been removed from my parent's home, when I was put into the foster care system. Perhaps the social worker hadn't believed me. It seemed Dad had perfected the art of making himself appear as a victim. The state of Louisiana—with all its swamps, Mardi Gras, and Cajun music—had taken the word of a child molester over that of children, one of whom had taken a hundred dollars of his own money to escape to the comfort of his sister.

My brother had been beaten his entire life, since he could walk. His small frame had been battered and kicked and had even cracked drywall, and yet he had been sent back into the hands of the very person who mistreated him. I put my face in my hands, knowing at that very moment my brother was probably being beaten. Years later, I would find out that, yes, he had been. Once again, I had let Bubba down. Who was I to gain the privilege to be safe and loved, but he couldn't?

MY FOSTER PARENTS HAD the idea that encouraging me to associate with other people would foster my integration with society. In all fairness, it should have, but it didn't.

Amy had been begging them to let her go on a date with a classmate, Greg. Finally, Kate and James said yes, but I was to accompany her on her first date. I needed to go out and have fun, they said, but I knew it was mainly because this was the only way they'd let Amy and Greg out on a date. I was fulfilling the need for a chaperone.

Greg arrived fifteen minutes early. He sauntered in with his hands stuffed in his green-and-white varsity jacket, his golden boy hair parted to the side, grinning nervously, while Kate smiled. She asked him a few questions like she was interviewing him for a job or to be president. Amy had already filled him in on what to say, and he answered like they'd rehearsed.

Yes, we're just going to eat out and to a movie.
No, we won't be doing anything else. Maybe we'll go to the park.
No, I don't drink.

After a few questions, Amy secretly motioned to me that it was time to hurry up. I started moving like Amy instructed, and we followed Greg to the car.

I hopped in the back, and as we were pulling out of the driveway, I started peppering them with questions about our evening plans. "Will we really have time to go to the park? What movie are we going to? I don't like horror movies. Can we eat first?" Amy waited until we were well down the road before she told me that they were dropping me off somewhere else.

"Wait, what?" I demanded. "You're ditching me with people I don't even know? I thought we were going to a movie. Take me back home."

Greg sped up; the passing houses became a blur.

"Oh, stop being such a baby," Amy teased. "I should have packed a diaper bag for you. You never go out. All you want to do is stay home, like a granny. I'm nice enough to bring you, and this is the thanks I get?" Amy then reached over and cranked up the music so loud that it did no good to speak.

Greg laughed in a disturbing way when she called me a granny, but when Amy glanced out the window, he turned and shot me an apologetic glance. He seemed to have some pity on me, but it did nothing to garner my respect for either of them. I'd been shanghaied onto this date and would have to spend the evening being party to a ruse concocted to fool my foster parents, something I didn't feel comfortable with.

I crossed my arms and took deep breaths. I felt like I was being used by Kate and James to spy on Amy, and I was being used by Amy to fool them. I didn't want to be a part of this. My anger built up long before we got to the ditching spot. It was a tiny wooden house with a sagging front porch and a small carport. I still wasn't talking to Amy. She'd culled a promise out of me, not to say anything to Kate. I could tell she didn't trust me, and I sure didn't trust her. But we were now in this together, whether I liked it or not.

We walked up the steps, Amy and Greg holding hands. One of her friends, Cathy, opened the door and hugged her. "Everything's planned out," she said. She motioned for us to come in.

It was an older home with paneling and lots of ceiling fans. A couple, probably in their fifties, were watching the news. Greg went into the living room with the adults, while Amy and I followed Cathy to her room. The walls were plastered with posters of New Kids on the Block and Def Leppard. The dresser had an Aqua Net-stained mirror on it and was completely littered with makeup and several bottles of Aqua Net hairspray. She and Amy kept spraying their hair and adding more makeup. Another girl walked in, and I heard some boys talking to Greg.

I decided to slip out of the room and go sit with the adults. The boys had drifted into the kitchen to talk. I introduced myself, hoping this was where I could stay for the rest of the evening. My mouth tasted like Aqua Net, and I found myself smacking my lips to get rid of the taste. The older gentleman flicked channels back and forth, between the fight of Mike Tyson and Tyrell Biggs, and a live report about a child who had fallen into a well.

Eighteen-month-old Jessica McClure had fallen down a twenty-two-foot well in her aunt's backyard. The story was captivating. She had been trapped in the well—which was only eight inches wide—for over fifty hours. The news report was slow-paced, but the boxing match was exciting, and I watched as Tyrell Biggs kept falling, taking punch after punch from Mike Tyson. It was just as painful to watch the fight as the baby trapped in the well.

Soon, Amy and Greg made an appearance, as though they were leaving. Amy didn't tell me where they were going, and I didn't ask. I glanced their way but rolled my eyes when I heard the door slap. Moments later, the Camaro fired up and squealed out the driveway.

I didn't care about them anymore and was completely immersed in the screen. By this time, the rest of the girls were sprayed down with Aqua Net, layered up with mascara, and ready to go somewhere, "riding" with the guys, so I had to leave the adults and the TV.

We piled into a red sportscar. Cathy's boyfriend, Matt, drove. The car slipped onto the highway. I'd never gone out with a group of people, or anyone really. It was chaotic. The commotion in the car was absurd, yet no one else appeared to be bothered by it. I seemed to be the only person who was spellbound by the blaring of rock music and the squealing of tires on pavement. As we sped through town, my ears were pummelled by the timbres of different voices in the car as they slashed and pricked the air, the instrumentals of Led Zeppelin and Metallica overpowered by teenage rage.

After a few hours of aggressively riding around, we met Amy and Greg in an empty parking lot, next to a bar called the Purple Peacock. Greg's eyes were bloodshot, and he was violently throwing empty beer bottles all over. He let out a loud *whoop* each time one hit the ground and threw his fists into air.

"What is wrong with Greg?" I demanded.

Amy said nothing.

"I'm done," I told her. "I'm calling Kate to pick me up."

I began to walk toward a payphone, but she seized my wrist.

"You aren't going anywhere," Amy said.

"I'm leaving. You and Greg have been drinking, and he looks drunk."

"You aren't going to ruin things for me!" she shouted. "I hate you. I knew from the moment I met you that I couldn't trust you."

"I just want to go home! I'm not your babysitter," I said.

"I let you come, and this is the thanks I get," she huffed.

"No, I was *forced* to come, and this is the thanks that *I* get."

Still holding my wrist, she gritted her teeth. "You know how they are. If you call them, I'll make your life miserable, Tracie, I swear."

I knew she would.

Amy extracted another promise out of me to say nothing. I stood on the shattered glass, the night lights sparkling in her glazed blue eyes, her promise to ruin my life glaring back at me. This was Amy's life, not mine. All the broken pieces we were standing on were of her world, not mine. I just wanted to go home, for Kate to comfort me, and I didn't want to walk on broken glass anymore. I wanted my freedom back, my dreams back. Another bottle came flying down near me, and I jumped as the fragments flew everywhere. Greg let out a wild shout and threw his empty hands in the air.

I remember staring at Greg, searching his face. He seemed different from just a few hours earlier, a whole other mood. *So violent.* I began to doubt myself, wondering why I was afraid. My mind, used to being self-soothed by quiet, was being clobbered. It felt like I was drowning in chaos. I wanted to go home to Kate. Then I remembered: Kate was the one who had pushed me to go.

I couldn't catch a clear grasp about that night, for months playing the events in my head over and over. I wondered if Greg's behavior had triggered something in me to frighten me so much it drove an even further wedge between me and Amy.

It would be answered almost two years later, when I'd walk through a series of metal detectors and steel doors that clanged shut behind me. I'd drop off a paper bag. I'd be led to a glass window with a chair and a phone receiver. Minutes later, Greg would appear, shackled, on the opposite side of the window. We took our phones off their cradles and put them to our ears. I told Greg I dropped off some things. He slumped in a chair on the other side of the glass and thanked me. His eyes were soft and watery. I asked him if anyone else came to visit him. He said only one other person, an aunt. He paused, then told me his fifteen-year-old brother's body had been preserved from the fire by a waterbed he fell into.

The stab marks were still there.

———

THE NEXT MORNING, KATE asked me to come with her to a store. As she and I were traveling alone in the van, she started probing me about the night before. What did we do? Where did we go? My story and Amy's didn't completely match up, apparently, and Amy had only briefed me vaguely on what I should say. I stared out the window, while Kate continued prodding me for a response. I realized she had only asked me to come to question me alone, and I wasn't in the mood for interrogation.

"You know, I had you followed by my friend CJ, who's a cop. He told me everything."

I studied Kate. Her face was serious. I didn't know how to read it. Kate was good at bluffing, better than I was. Her probing continued. Finally, I decided to come clean and tell her about some of the events, although I wasn't foolish enough to spill my guts about everything. I still didn't know what Kate knew, and I certainly didn't trust Amy. If things didn't go right, I could be the one to get the boot.

"I don't know where Amy and Greg went. They dropped me off somewhere and left."

———

"WHAT DID YOU TELL them?" Amy demanded the next day. "I'm being punished because of you! I never did like you." She stormed away.

Monday, at school, there was a different attitude among our mutual acquaintances. At lunch, I sat at a table with the usual group of people, and every one of them picked up their trays and carried them to another table. Walking down the hall afterward, a couple of Amy's friends, including Greg, walked by me. One of them stuck his leg out and tripped me. My books and papers flew as I landed, face first, on the concrete floor. I looked up to see Greg laughing, ambling away.

Amy started getting off the bus a block away from our stop, loudly expressing in front of the entire bus that she didn't want to be seen getting off the bus with me. "If y'all want to sit by a snitch, she's over there," she hollered. From then on, I had trouble finding a seat. No one wanted to sit by the snitch.

During one English class, the teacher finished early and allowed us free time to do as we pleased. Amy sat behind me in that class. My heart dropped into my stomach as I heard all the desks behind me pulling away. I turned to see that I was alone, and Amy had her finger pointed at me, laughing. I put my head down and closed my eyes, pretending to sleep, so I didn't have to see her anymore.

Occasionally, Amy spoke loud enough for me to hear. "I hate living with a snitch." I knew she did it on purpose, but I resolved to keep to myself. I had no one to tell anyway. If I told Kate, she would punish Amy, who would just make my life even more miserable. My life had taken such a drastic turn. It went from being sublime to tiptoeing through my room looking for hidden mines. I became rattled by the belief that I could do nothing right, and every time I was in Amy's presence, I discerned slivers of hatred toward me coupled with evil intentions.

I decided that the world was a little more complex than I had originally thought.

EACH AFTERNOON, I FOUND myself sulking and withdrawing from Kate and James. They both seemed to be giving me the cold shoulder and spoke in hushed tones when I walked into a room. Somehow, I had become the black sheep of the family, while Amy heaped beatings on me at night as I tried to sleep.

One morning, I found Amy staring at me, already dressed and ready for school, with a giant smile. We didn't speak, but I wondered what she was up to. I got ready for school as Amy watched me, which made me uneasy. After I was dressed and ready, Amy informed me that Kate wanted to speak with me. I knew things were shaky, so maybe they'd tell me Amy was leaving and our lives could finally get back to normal.

Amy lingered in the hall, like a greasy odor lingers in a kitchen long after you've cooked. Kate and James were sitting in bed, Kate still with her nightgown on. Her expression was stretched—cold, tired—as if she hadn't slept well. The air had a somber tone about it.

"We've been talking," she began, "and we think it's time that you go. Your grades have declined, you sleep in class, you and Amy don't get along, and this is getting very stressful. It just isn't working out."

I was completely thrown and didn't know what to say. I glanced over at Amy, who'd moved closer into the room, acting completely thunderstruck.

"I sleep in class? What are you talking about?"

"Amy told us you sleep, not paying attention. That's why your grades are suffering. You don't care."

From the corner of my eye, I saw Amy standing in the doorway.

"No, that's not true."

"Amy told us everything."

"But—"

Kate put her hand to her head and closed her eyes.

James said, "Go pack your things, now."

I felt like some part of me was going to erupt. I had worked too hard to get here. *No!* I wanted to scream. But I wasn't a strong enough person to do that, and only stood, suffocating on my deep sobs. The room twisted; faces began to warp. Odd specks of light began to dot the air as I crumpled to the floor.

I heard Kate say something and I pulled myself up, the room spinning like a vortex. The dots floated in front of my face. No one offered to help me. I glanced at Amy, but she saw the look on my face and fled. I stumbled to my room. My entire body was shaking so badly I felt like I would shatter in a million different particles and dissipate in the air.

I collapsed on the bed, still not understanding why I was leaving. I wailed deep, bottomless-pit sobs punctuated by pauses only long enough to inhale more air, before starting up again. My head thrummed. Why was I so upset? God had held up his end of the deal. I'd found the loving family I had walked half my life for. I would find another place just as nice, maybe better. That didn't make my head hurt any less.

I sat up on the bed, looking around the room, trying to compose one last memory. I remember the pale light of the walk-in closet, the coolness of the sheets under my palms, a book I had been reading lying face down, opened to create a pyramid. And Amy, in the open doorway, grinning like a Cheshire Cat.

I walked out the room and into the kitchen. My brain was spinning in my skull. I went to the cabinet for some aspirin. I poured a bunch in my hand. I popped two in my mouth and put the rest in my pocket. The door was cracked open, so I slipped outside and settled onto the wooden swing, staring at the unkempt plot of land across the street. I didn't want to leave. The empty lot with long sprigs of dying grass was as unfriendly as ever, but I didn't want to leave.

As I trudged back to my room, I was cornered by Amy, who asked what I was doing.

"Are you following me?" I accused, then told her to go away. For the first time, ever, she listened to me and slipped into Kate's room. I crawled back into bed and closed my eyes. I wasn't going to school. I was awakened shortly by Kate. Her face was grave, her voice stern. "Did you take some aspirin?"

"Yes."

"I just bought that bottle. They're almost gone." Her eyes were serious.

I didn't want to tell Kate that I stole them, but then I thought maybe I could use this to my advantage. I remembered how my aunt had sobbed when Josephine and my dad pranked her. This could work. I told Kate I swallowed them.

My spur of the moment scheme was already starting to unravel. I wasn't as good at this as I thought I'd be. Panic began to overtake me. The only time I had ever lied to Kate was when Amy told me to.

Kate didn't caress my face. Instead, she stomped out the room. James said I'd taken most of them.

Kate shouted, "This why I'm sending her away!"

My heart dropped for what felt like several stories, as though it was the ball dropping in Times Square on New Year's Eve.

I didn't care what they thought. I hoped they thought I was dying. Maybe they would see how upset I was and give me another chance.

They didn't.

They took me to the hospital, instead, while Amy took the bus to school. When we entered the hospital, I slipped the pills out of my pocket, into a trash can. I decided that this might buy me some time. Maybe I could talk to Kate and James alone. But that didn't work out either; they ignored me. Kate was steamed and told me to stop talking. The doctor made me swallow some stuff that tasted like charcoal and made me want to vomit. I said I was fine, but no one listened to me. James said he had to go to work and left, without saying goodbye.

Marla showed up at the hospital and said it was time to go. She was taking me to another hospital. "This one is fine. As a matter of fact, I don't even need to be here," I told her. "I didn't even take the pills. I tossed them."

Marla and Kate glanced at each other, then Marla motioned for us to leave. Kate went to her van and came back with a black trash bag filled with my clothes. She dropped it at my feet.

Trash Bag Tracie.

"This is how it's going to end?" I asked. "I don't mean anything to you?"

Kate studied her feet and said nothing.

I looked longingly at Kate as she turned to walk off and imagined her going back to Amy. I pictured everyone at home—which was no longer my home—sitting on the sofa that evening talking about me, what a horrible foster child I had been, failing math. James would crack open his Bible and read something aloud. He'd talk about unconditional love and forgiveness. Then everyone would turn in for the night, without me.

Over a quarter century later, in a phone conversation, Amy would tell me that the bad grades had been the reason I was sent away. She told me I should have picked up my algebra grade, at least. "It terrified me," she told me. "It made me study harder so I wouldn't be sent away too." I remembered how many times I ignored Mr. Schultz, picked up my books, and walked out of his class because he called me Lion. How variables reminded me of an algebra book Dad bought me when I was in the third grade. How I despised algebra and for the rest of my life would never use it again.

I heard my name and snapped in the direction it came from. My eyes settled on Marla.

"It's over, Tracie," she said. "Let's go."

The realization sank into me that I was being tossed out like trash. I was getting the big kiss-off. Marla shrugged and motioned for me to get into the car. I glanced back at Kate one more time, looking for the opportunity to give her a hug, but she was almost to her van. I stepped into Marla's car and snapped my seat belt into place. I asked why we were going to a different hospital because I felt fine.

"It's not the kind of hospital you're thinking of Tracie. It's a mental hospital."

"Seriously?" I shouted. "You think I'm crazy? You have no idea what's been going on."

"I know you're failing school again, and you just took a bunch of pills to kill yourself."

"I need a tutor. And for the last time, I only took a few aspirin," I said. "It was a *prank*."

"I heard you were an honor-roll student. Suddenly you need a tutor?"

I rolled my eyes. "Someone not trapped in foster care would have been *offered* a tutor," I said. "I got offered the door. How do you think I feel?"

"Listen, it's just for a few days. I can't find a bed for you. I really don't have a choice. Most foster homes don't take teenagers. They take in young children because they're more manageable. You really caught me off guard with this."

"I'm manageable. Wait, caught *you* off guard?"

"Yes, you should try to be more like Amy."

We drove farther away from the place I had called home for six months. By now, it was late afternoon, and the sun was starting to set in the west, behind us. I mashed my eyelids together and tried not to sob. I felt like such an idiot because, being a Neanderthal sporting a safari shirt, I had tried to blend in with a normal family. I wiped tears from my eyes as I realized I had thought I belonged. Amy, on the other hand, had waltzed in with shimmering eyes, like it was her star performance, and she was already up for an Academy Award. Of course she belonged. She didn't travel with a shovel. There was nothing I could do; it was now Amy's world. I stared at the blurred scenery outside the passenger window as Marla drove me to mine.

Chapter 14:

Molly

—

We pulled up to a building that was several stories tall. I hoisted my trash bag over my shoulder. I was led to an elevator that took us to the fourth floor. After we stepped off the elevator, two double doors sealed the entrance to the corridor. Marla pressed a button. They swung open. I shuffled in. The doors clanged shut behind us. We continued down the hall, to a room that was thronged with people. Bright light spilled in through a tall window at the end of the other hall, sopping up any darkness trying to leave.

The first thing I noticed was this place was not kidding around. It was full of real live crazy people, close enough for me to touch. Some of them moved with paralyzed sluggishness and spoke in thick, suffocated voices. I appraised the room. My eyes settled on a gray-haired woman smoking in a corner. She wore a red hat with a feather, and a handful of fake diamond and emerald rings sparkled when she moved. I stood transfixed and could not take my eyes off her. She sat quietly, blowing smoke on the people around her, who also sat quietly doing the same thing.

"Is she a crazy person?" I whispered to Marla, but she ignored me.

A few heads turned in my direction. I looked at the ceiling, the walls, the speckled linoleum, anything to avoid eye contact. It was critical that I did not lock eyes with them, or I would turn crazy too. A few nurses in white outfits sat on the other side of a glass window behind computers, amidst a sea of reports, hastily banging their fingers on keyboards or scratching pens on paper.

When Marla was done signing some paperwork, it was clear that she was itching to leave and told me that she would be back for me in a few days. She waved goodbye and left me standing, anchored by my trash bag, as I stared around at all the crazy people. They came and inspected me from all sides, like a mouse in a field being circled by hawks. A man with rotten teeth walked about, arguing with himself about the weather.

There were a lot of depressed-looking people in the room, most of them older. No one was my age, or anywhere near it. Almost everyone was on medication, I would soon learn. Some wanted to take it and hurriedly rushed to get it, while others crossed their arms and refused. Those were the crazy ones. I would learn to stay away from them.

I stood amid all the craziness with my bag. At first, I was confused about why I was there. Marla had told me there weren't a lot of beds for teenage girls, that all the group homes were full, even the juvenile delinquent homes—which startled me because it made me realize she considered putting me in a juvenile home.

Am I a criminal? A threat to society?

Clutching my trash bag, I waited quietly, observing my new surroundings. The walls were faded and dim from years of smokers. There were no pictures or posters, no words of encouragement anywhere. Blank, smoky walls. I hated the smell of cigarette smoke, and here I stood breathing it, choking on its thickness.

I was still fascinated by my surroundings, when a woman in a long white lab coat and creamy shoes approached me. She looked to be in her early forties and had short, bobbed hair. Her voice was warm, like a ray of light. She placed a gentle hand on my shoulder and led me to my room to put away my things. I wasn't allowed in the room during the day, she explained, and it would remain locked. There were four beds total in the room. Mine was closest to the window, which ran the length of the wall.

We settled on the bed and talked as though we were old friends. Her name was Molly.

She asked how old I was and when I replied that I was sixteen, she said that her daughter was the same age. Somehow, this fact was comforting for both of us. Molly told me that I would only be there for a few days, but she would look out for me. I nodded, not sure why I needed to be looked out for. After a few moments of silence, she placed her hand on my back and led me out the door, locking it behind us.

———

THE DAYS WERE LONG. Marla didn't come back for me in a day or two as promised, nor did she contact me to see how I was doing. The only phone I had access to was a payphone, but I had been left with no money. That also meant I couldn't buy soap, shampoo, or snacks. Kate had delivered me a few things in the trash bag, but they didn't last long. Someone in my room stole some of my things, so I was left with nothing for personal hygiene.

Most people left within two weeks, so the person who stole my soap, deodorant, and shampoo was long gone, before I finally couldn't stand the smell of myself anymore. I called Molly over one day, sobbing because I hated how I smelled. "What can I do?" I asked through tears.

I had bathed and brushed my teeth every day of my entire life, and here I was smelling like a dumpster. Molly told me not to worry and later came back with a bag of toiletries that she'd brought from her home. I felt guilty but grateful that she was looking out for me.

The cafeteria food was worse than the food at school, so I just picked at it. Since I arrived with no money for snacks from the vending machines to help curb my appetite, I gambled for it. I learned to play poker, blackjack, rummy, gin rummy, spades, crazy eights, Mississippi mud, and—one I already knew—go fish. We played for smokes in the common area. Someone gave me a few to get me started so I could join in the fun, though I regarded it more as a business. I won lots of smokes and traded them for candy, chips, or soda. I hoarded the smokes like currency. It was the only control I had.

I became obsessed with gambling and probably should have been locked away for it. Not all my hands were good. As a matter of fact, most were not. I knew how to bluff, how to win with the bad hands as well as the good ones. Giant Head Jimmy—a guy with a head way too big for his body—said that I looked like one of the faces on Mount Rushmore when I played cards. Stone cold. This was my only advantage. I wasn't lying about the cards that I held, just not letting on how bad they really were.

Sometimes I let an unlit cigarette dangle off my lip and pretended I was Amy. Maybe I would be a little cooler, accepted like she was. I secretly imagined that I was back with my foster parents, smoking, drinking with Greg, and making fun of everyone with Amy. Had I done that, I wouldn't be locked up. I never felt the need to light the cigarette that hung from my lip. Pretending had always been my reality. I would feign a mammoth drag to blend in with the others, but then I'd nearly choke on the smoke around me. A nurse always came along and ripped it from my mouth, to rip me back to reality.

Every afternoon, one nurse, Maria, would push a small metal cart loaded down with various bottles of pills out into the general area. Then she would yell, "Pill time!" and a collective mumble would follow as people awkwardly formed a line. I was already learning how to take vitals from the nurses so, after lots of begging on my part, Maria finally relented and allowed me to help dispense the drugs to the patients. She would read a patient's name from a list, and I'd nudge their little cup of pills toward them, as officially as if I had a PhD in pill pushing. I told Maria that I would like to be a nurse one day. After all, I'd get to have my own private parking space and drive a Mercedes-Benz. She told me, however, that as a nurse I would also be exposed to vomit and diarrhea, so I decided to give up on that career choice. There probably was a better way to get a good parking space.

My bond with the nurses became strong. Each one held special meaning to me. There were no male nurses; the only men were orderlies who tackled patients and stabbed them with needles. At first, I was shocked when I witnessed such a thing, but after a few times, I just watched the whole thing play out like a cheap movie. Abnormal was once again becoming my normal.

There was one lady who got stabbed with the needles, like it was a necessary part of her day. She screamed wild things and stood on top of the toilet to pee. Sometimes she ran out with no clothes on, her multiple layers of fat bouncing, and the orderlies ran to stab her with needles. Fortunately, she was only there for two weeks.

Each day, I perched on the windowsill at the end of the hallway, my arms shackled around my legs, my chin resting on my knees, solemnly watching the people below. Families. I often imagined I was with them, that the packages they carried were for me. Once, a stray dog passed, and I got so excited I loped off the windowsill and begged a nurse to go get it. She laughed at first, but then her face suddenly became serious. She shook her head as it dawned on her that I considered this my home.

My prayers almost halted. When I did pray, I whispered them into the night, before I fell asleep. It wasn't that I didn't want to believe anymore. For the first time in my life, I had cigarettes under my bed. I played poker and blackjack. I had been hit on by almost every man in the building. I had been groped in my sleep by a woman with ugly teeth who peed on my clean clothes. Molly had taken them home and washed them for me.

I'd gotten so used to the craziness that I slept right through it.

———

THANKSGIVING WEEK, THE NURSES asked me if I had anywhere to go. Had I heard from my social worker? Had they found me a home yet? Would Kate and James bring me to their house for Thanksgiving? I always shook my head. On Thanksgiving Day, I sat in a mental institution by myself, staring out the window. Even the homeless people who had been there the day before had someplace to go. I hadn't heard from Marla since she dropped me off. I had no one who wanted to be with me. I wasn't old enough to be homeless yet, but the conversation about "aging out" of foster care and being homeless tumbled around in my head, like clothes in a dryer. I might be homeless someday, but worse than regular homeless people. In the end, even they had someplace to go.

Somewhere out there, beyond the big glass window at the end of the corridor, was a world full of people, refusing me. My thoughts grew dark, and my heart grew darker. Light was having a harder time filtering into my soul, and I was getting tired of chasing tiny beacons. For the first time in my life, I was losing faith. That frightened me more than anything ever before. If I lost faith, I lost all hope. Hope was the only thing separating me from being homeless. I still had something left inside of me, and I had to use it.

Losing my first foster home did not sit well with me. It seemed like a bad omen for things that were yet to come, like I wasn't *refined* enough to be a part of a family or society. Looking at my surroundings, it was obvious I wasn't.

Living with strangers and adjusting to a fast-paced world were just a couple of things I hadn't been prepared for. Mostly, I hadn't been prepared for the feeling of heartbreak. Leaning against the window, I took my right shoe off and pulled up the inner sole. I still had my Latin phrase, although the words were fading. There was another tiny sheet of paper I had placed in there months earlier. It wasn't a prayer, but an expression of gratitude.

Thank you, God, for James and Kate.

I forgot I had written that in the days before Amy. I pushed my Latin one back in my shoe but kept the other one out. I trudged to a lighter hanging from a chain, which patients used to light their cigarettes. A nurse looked up from her desk, frowning, because she knew I didn't smoke. As I set the paper on fire, she jerked up to stop me, but she wasn't quick enough. I turned around and held the paper at arm's length, while she ran for some water. By the time she arrived, it was too late.

The paper was ashes, and I was probably crazy now.

There was nothing left of my fire but a little curl of smoke. Maybe I was crazy for believing so much, but I had to believe there was more to life than this.

The nurse reprimanded me, and I went back to my seat on the window and stared into the empty streets, my soles nearly as empty.

I DIDN'T CALL THEM crazy anymore, the people within those walls. They had become more real to me as I learned their thoughts and feelings. They were people with real stories. Each had their own tale, and I didn't think anyone had ever taken the time to hear them before. I taught myself to listen with such lucidity that I could feel the emotions in their words, *feel* their stories.

There was one guy I kept an eye on. One day, as I was walking behind him, I noticed him glance peculiarly from side to side, appearing agitated. Suddenly, he reached for a large wooden chair, and within seconds I was tackled to the floor. I heard the *swoosh* of the chair passing through the air over me, then it slammed into the wall. I lay crumpled on the floor, with someone lying on top of me, protecting me. I should have known anything was possible here.

As the chair splintered into dozens of pieces, I instinctively covered my face. He had missed me by only a few inches. He had targeted me because of my age: I was by far the youngest, and he saw how the nurses were protective of me. He wanted out, and I was his ticket.

Several orderlies jumped on top of him, restraining him and stabbing him rapidly with needles. Two nurses quickly grabbed me and ushered me to the protective confines of my room. I was in shock as they shut the door behind them. Then, I heard a click of the lock. It was at that time that I remembered I was at an institution for the insane. Was I insane too? Was I worse than the child molesters and rapists? The arsonists? The angry people who smashed chairs against walls? Oh, I hoped not. I don't know where they took that guy, but I never saw him again. Immediately, I knew my time was going to be cut short. Molly had been telling me it wasn't a safe place for me, and it wasn't a home. She asked me regularly if I'd heard from the social worker. I told her I had no way of contacting her. Molly wanted me out, and I wanted in.

It was comforting, knowing that the staff was looking out for me, trying to protect me from the violent patients and the child molesters. But I hadn't made it this far to hide under quilts or lock myself in a room. I was going to face them, face the whole wide world—have a real Mexican stand-off if I had to—and stare them down into the ground, for everything my dad did to me. The threats had increased, but so had my strength. I decided to focus my energies on being less of a teenage girl and more of a warrior.

One evening, Molly caught me alone and gave me some fudge. She winked. "Don't tell anyone I gave you that." Between fudgy bites, she said, "So, what are your plans? What are you going to do when you get out?" I looked outside, not sure what I would do. I was different now. I never thought my life could be harder than it was with my family, but it was. Somehow, the world found a way to constrict me, just a little tighter. This hospital, with all its craziness and insanity, had become my blanket. I felt safe there, safer than I had felt in a long time. But now I was different, and I knew it. Molly realized it too.

It dawned on me that I was shedding the childhood I had tried so desperately to hang on to. I mentioned it to Molly. "It's kind of funny that I had to come to a mental institution to find out that the whole wide world is crazy."

Molly's eyes glazed over. I wanted to tell her the rest of my thoughts but decided to keep them to myself, as I saw her studying me.

I wanted to tell her, "*You know what can drive a person insane? Walking in faith for almost eight years, hoping somebody will love you one day.*" I ended up in a mental institution, and still nobody loved me. Except for the child molester sitting in the corner, slowly inhaling a Marlboro, while gazing intently at me. He loved me.

I DIDN'T LIKE IT when Molly worked the night shift because I didn't get to see much of her. Lights had to be out by nine, and she arrived around that time. One night, when I knew she was working, I loped out of bed after everyone in my room was asleep. I peeked out to look for Molly. When I didn't see anyone, I walked into the hallway.

"What are you doing?" I heard a familiar voice ask, playfully.

"Oh, hey," I said in my pretend-surprise voice. "What are you doing here?"

Peering from around a corner, Molly suspiciously raised one eyebrow and waved me over. "Come on, we're about to watch a movie. Do you want some popcorn?"

The other two nurses saw me and smiled. One moved over so I could sit. "Thanks," I said, "but I'm sitting by Molly."

When Molly came back with the popcorn, we took our seats in the long row of chairs. "Now, remember," she whispered, "this is our secret. You aren't supposed to be up, and I don't want everyone else thinking they can get up too. They already say I spoil you. After the movie, you have to go back to bed." She gave me a little wink and clicked on the movie. I took a handful of popcorn and smiled from ear to ear. Molly always made exceptions for me. The movie turned out to be R-rated, and I got laughed at when I closed my eyes and covered my ears. One of the orderlies, George, said, "You don't have to do that. Your mama and daddy aren't here to tell you what to do."

"Oh, but I have better standards than my parents," I quickly replied.

After the movie was over, Molly told me I should probably go to bed. I just stared at her while slowly crunching on more popcorn. I wasn't going anywhere.

"Let's dance," she said, finally giving up.

"Okay," I said, standing up. "This should be interesting."

"You ever dance with a boy?" She grinned.

"No." My face flushed deep red.

"Why not?"

"Oh, I don't know. I can't dance."

Molly shook her head and chuckled. "I see you dancing here. You're the leader of the pack."

"I can do crazy dance moves that mean nothing, or dance by myself, but never with another person, especially not with a... Anyway, I don't know how."

"Tracie, you have to meet boys one day and go out, and then you'll dance. Come on, I'll show you."

Molly took my hands, and I awkwardly pressed mine into hers.

"Loosen up. I'll show you, but you have to promise to get a date with a boy when you leave here."

I nodded with hesitation, knowing good and well I wouldn't.

She held my hands as we danced together, and she patiently trained me not to step all over her creamy white shoes. We laughed together and joked about how I could move to California, smash grapes with my feet, and never, ever dance with a boy I liked, unless he enjoyed having broken feet.

Laughing, she reached over and hugged me, holding me tightly. She told me I reminded her of her daughter, Tricia. As she held me, I wished I was Tricia and could go home with her at the end of her shift, instead of staying locked up like a prisoner. Molly and Maria had already both told me that they'd asked their husbands if I could live with them, but neither had met me and both said no.

I knew Molly felt sorry for me because I was the same age as her daughter, but this didn't feel like a pity hug. It felt like she really cared about me. In those moments, I was her daughter. Her other daughter. It was just me and her, and I was in heaven, dancing in a pair of mismatched socks.

Chapter 15:

The Prize and the Pain

The next day, I was walking toward my room, when Giant Head Jimmy motioned me over. He was standing near a closet, and as I got close, he slowly pulled a set of keys out of his pocket. They belonged to Roxy, the lady who cleaned. He held the keys out to me and placed them in my hand, curling my fingers over them so no one would see. He then leaned in and whispered, "These are yours to do with what you want." As he walked off, he gave me a wink.

I didn't want to stand by the door, in case Roxy came back, so I secretly slipped the keys into my pocket and walked away. That day, I found myself staring at the steel doors, knowing that I had the keys to freedom. I could run faster than all of the nurses. I could have my life back and restart my journey to California.

Molly came to meet me. "What's bothering you?" she asked, poking me in the side.

"Nothing."

"Why are you just sitting here, staring outside?"

"You have to promise you won't be mad."

"I promise."

"Put your hand out."

Molly extended her hand to me. I placed the keys in her hand. She stared into her open palm, her lips tense, face taut. I thought she would be happy, but she was disappointed, instead. "You know, I expect this from the others, but not from you. We've been looking for this set. Roxy was the one who misplaced them. She could have lost her job. You owe her an apology. I forgive you, but I'm disappointed."

I didn't know what I felt most guilty about: the fact that Roxy could have lost her job, or the fact that I didn't want to leave.

"Molly?"

"Yes?"

"Am I crazy?"

It was a stupid question. I knew I wasn't crazy. I'd been raised to study hard, to obey the laws of man, to walk a chalk line so thin, it was impossible not to be perfect. I wasn't crazy. My dad, who claimed to be the most perfect man of them all, had raised me.

Molly leaned in close and grinned, "Of course you are. We all are."

AS THE MONTHS PASSED, I got used to the opening and closing of the big doors at the end of the corridor, the slow creak they made when opened, the giant slamming when they closed. I no longer looked to see who was coming or going. Whoever it was at the end of the long corridor that swallowed the darkness was somebody nobody wanted.

Technically, Kate and James were still my foster parents until a new home could be found, so they came to bring me some clothes a week before Christmas. When I was alone with Amy, she told me that Kate bought me clearance items as gifts. She went on to say that Kate got her some name brand clothing, more than she was expecting.

"I wouldn't be caught dead in the clothes you got." Amy giggled. "The housecoat she got you is a man's and pops open in the front. Mama Kate accidentally bought me one, too, but she took it back and got me a more feminine one that buttons in the front."

I held the housecoat up to examine it. It was navy blue with a strap.

"You call her Mama?" I asked.

"Sure," she replied. "We've gotten a lot closer since you left."

The door squeaked, and I looked up to see a guy poking his head in. I hollered at him to get out.

"This place is so gross—full of creeps and perverts. I hope they find you a nice home like I have," Amy said, then walked away.

Molly took the clothes home with her to wash, but the legs on the jeans twisted in a weird way and one of the sleeves on the shirt shrank badly. I told her I didn't want the clothes but hated to throw them away. She told me that I could donate them to other patients. I donated it all, including the man's housecoat.

Christmas Day came, and once again, I was by myself. Molly came from her house to spend about an hour with me. She delivered me a few trinket gifts, and a metal container of cookies she had baked. As always, she made the walls less lonely. She said she wished she could bring me home, but I told her not to worry about it. She hugged me before she left.

I was grateful her family had loaned her to me, if only for an hour. It felt like ages since I had fled my home by walking the tracks and started my life over again. It was as if I had decided to shed my childhood skin to take care of myself, but everyone kept interfering. And maybe I let them. Maybe I still wanted to be a child.

I pressed my hand to the cool glass window and imagined myself being all alone in the world. Then, I looked around at the empty hall and general room and remembered: I already was.

———

FACES CHANGED CONSTANTLY. I had been locked up longer than any other patient ever had been. This was not a long-term facility; the average patient stayed only a week or two. An arsonist who had burned down several buildings was there for two weeks. The hardcore rapists, thieves, and child molesters sometimes stayed longer, perhaps three or four weeks. Three of them had cornered me and rubbed or pressed their bodies up against me. One snuck into the women's restroom while I was showering, and another consistently snuck into my bedroom while I was napping, once holding a serrated knife to my throat, threatening me not to scream. Luckily, someone noticed and ran in behind him, just as he folded and slipped the knife back into his pocket. Molly locked me in after that and ordered the other nurses to do so as well. I was offered pot by one of the men who was there for drug addiction. Someone visiting him had brought it in. There were others there for bipolar disorder, although they usually remained the shortest time since all they needed was medication. I had been there for over four months, and not once had I heard from a social worker. Eleven child molesters came and went. Slowly, I was learning to fit into the adult world. Just smile and pretend everything was okay. Pretend to care for the very people who wanted to hurt you, who *were* hurting you. Feel their pain instead of yours.

I learned quickly that this place was a dumping ground. In the beginning of my solo journey away from my family, I was trying to escape from only one man who couldn't keep his hands off me. Now, I was surrounded by a dozen—locked in close quarters with them. Daily, I had to face what

I used to believe I'd escaped, as my childhood was shredded by chaos. There were days on the window ledge when I craned to see the sun dipping between a pair of buildings—a golden reminder of my childhood—and could feel the warmth on the glass. I imagined I was eight again, skipping between rails. Life had been easy then, and I hadn't even known it.

Still, there was a familiarity being there: random objects hurled through the air; men pacing with their eyes narrowed; me, cloaking my face with a book, pretending I was somewhere else. It was as familiar as being home. I expected Bubba to pop in at any moment, and say, "Whatcha doing?"

It was Monday morning, just after breakfast, and everyone was gathered in the main room for group session. Molly had already told me I wasn't allowed to participate because I was a minor, but I still had to sit every morning and read a book, quietly. Normally, the nurse began by asking everyone in the circle to share their feelings. A man started about how he shouldn't be there. He became enraged, then he started sobbing. I'd gotten used to this type of behavior. It reminded me of my dad, only I never saw him cry.

I was staring at a book, half listening, when the nurse spoke in a low, monotone voice. She detailed symptoms of a mental illness called borderline personality disorder: fear of abandonment, unstable relationships, extreme emotional swings, explosive anger, and feeling suspicious or out of touch with reality. My head snapped in her direction and my ears fine-tuned the nurse's speech. Every word she laid out described my dad. Exactly.

I remember tilting my head in confusion. He couldn't be mentally ill. He was a truck driver. He delivered people's packages. People *liked* him. I jiggled my head back and forth to knock my brain around a little, so I would come to my senses, but instead, I started laughing manically inside my head.

What I was hearing was just a coincidence.

I flicked through the book. Dad's multiple moods charged through my mind. I remembered when I was five years old. Dad was navigating the car through different neighborhoods, his eyes searching driveways. Mom was seated next to him, while Bubba and I played with baseball cards on the back seat.

I heard Dad tell Mom to look for old car batteries people put out. I don't remember why, but there must have been some type of value to them. About a half hour into our trip, I told Dad I needed to pee. At first, he said nothing. I peered over the seat, searching for an answer. Moments later, he turned toward me and shouted, "Tell your mother to get her boyfriend to cup his hands, so you can pee in them!"

I looked at Mom. She didn't have a boyfriend. She begged him to stop. He became enraged, reaching over to hit her with his fist. He began yelling more about the non-existent boyfriend with imaginary hands I was supposed to pee in. I leaned back and pushed the baseball cards aside. The fight became more violent. He hit her repeatedly, then continued driving.

I peed on the seat.

It was just a coincidence. Wasn't it?

Wouldn't it be ironic if he committed all these crimes against me—destroyed my life—and I ended up being the one locked up for it? That would be insane. I deserved to be there. I wasn't a good daughter. I failed algebra. I fought him when no one else would. By the time the group session was over, I'd convinced myself that everything that happened to me was my fault. I tossed the book aside. I wanted to stand up and shout out loud. My dad wasn't crazy. *I was.*

THERE SEEMED TO BE an awful lot of homeless people coming in on very cold nights. The shelters were full, so they went to a hospital and feigned mental illness, so they could get a warm bed, free TV, and meals for a week or so. Then, when the weather warmed, they were miraculously better, thanked the nurses for their services, and left until the next cold spell. I knew this because one homeless man, Sam, told me that he was professionally crazy, that being homeless was his career.

"Not to brag," he said, "but I haven't worked a day in over twenty years."

I learned a lot from him, as he explained the many perks to being homeless. There was no other place on earth you could go and meet such a diverse group of people, he told me. "Just look around," he said.

My eyes scanned the main general area. There was a dusky man named Edward, who told everyone he was from Africa, but he was really from six blocks away. A young Caucasian woman, named Carrie, who was twirling like a ballerina up and down the main hall. And Sung-ho, from South Korea—he was the main reason Molly locked me in my room—rubbing his hands together and waggling his eyebrows at me.

Sam was particularly smart, because when he wasn't in a mental hospital, he hung around the public library and read. He knew interesting things, like how our brains float around in our heads and how a little bit of liquor is called a noggin. He seemed to know an unusual amount of information about heads and what goes on in there.

Sam helped me to brush up on my Latin, which I hadn't studied in almost two years. I pulled the old slip of paper out of my shoe and showed him the Latin phrase that I'd had written in there for years.

Dum vita est spes est.

Sam smiled and said that I was very bright for my age and that when I was homeless, I should visit the public library—that I could read and study all day for free. He told me how I could find shelter and that I could keep coming here every few months if the shelters were full.

"I think I'm homeless now," I told him.

"The library is the place to go," he said. "And maybe one day you'll be as smart as me."

I didn't want to think about staying in shelters or going to the library for warmth and knowledge. Sam knew how to spin a good yarn, but I wanted none of this. He was smart enough to be a doctor because he could speak Latin—I milked what information I could from him—but he chose to be in a mental institution. I didn't want to spend the rest of my life there, but that was where Molly was, so I wasn't going to buck the system. I realized, though, that one day, I would need to leave and would never, ever come back.

I would leave with a consolation gift, however: the knowledge that all good things come to an end. Maybe life is a series of random chances and fate doesn't exist at all. I didn't get the gift, until I reaped the benefit of my own faith. It hurt more, having it for a short time and losing it, than never having it at all. The prize is fleeting, and the pain is infinite.

THE DAY FINALLY CAME when Molly reached my social worker and demanded that she pick me up. That night, as I sat on my bed staring into the inky sky that was slowly filling up with storm clouds, my door creaked open.

"You are less stressed here," a voice said.

I turned. It was Molly. I asked her what she was talking about. Molly walked toward me and sat down on the bed next to me. She told me she noticed something different about me, a metamorphosis.

"You seemed so adamant about pleasing everyone when you got here, as though you needed to be perfect. Now, you are much more relaxed, as though a great weight has been lifted off you."

I didn't know how to respond, so I continued staring out the window.

Was I more relaxed?

Molly's voice softened. "You said you are afraid of failing on the outside," she said. "Inside these walls, you laugh, dance, make jokes. You aren't crazy," she continued as she gently took my hand. "You are comfortable in it."

"I'm a failure out there," I told her. "It's pretty hard to fail here." I grinned to lighten up the moment.

Molly smiled back. "You aren't a failure. You just need someone to believe in you."

"Molly?"

"Yes?"

"Amy won."

"She won what?"

"She won life."

"No, Tracie," Molly said as she gently stroked my hair. "She didn't."

Molly wrapped her arm around me and held me as we both gazed out the window, into the sky and the faint smattering of stars that weren't hidden behind gray clouds. We both knew why I was sad.

I'd been in the mental hospital for over five months. Molly had been the most stable, kind person in my life, and now I had to leave her. This would be my last night, and I had mixed feelings about it. Molly's friendly smiles, soft hugs, and the warmth of my bed in front of the window, were a guaranteed promise every day. But now I was going to have to start over again. Lightning bolts split across the sky, trailed by claps of thunder. It felt as though the earth and heavens were battling over my destiny.

Molly and I waited for the storm, together.

Chapter 16:

The Dungeon

It was pouring rain the morning Marla picked me up. Molly came, though it was her day off, to say goodbye. It was one of the hardest moments of my life. Then I heaved my trash bag and followed Marla down the long stairwell, wondering if Molly was still at the top, listening to my footsteps.

I tossed my garbage bag of clothes into the back seat of Marla's car. As we drove away, a blurred Molly watched from the window, her hand pressed against the glass. I stared at that window, until it was no longer in sight.

Marla and I followed a dark convoy of gray clouds, down an interstate, in the direction I originally ran away from. After about forty-five minutes, we turned off and within minutes entered a neighborhood, getting closer to my new home—the one that had taken Marla almost six months to find and was located only seven miles from where my parents lived.

My social worker silently slipped her finger over the door lock button. I pretended not to notice, but it certainly didn't help to ease me. In my first year of foster care, I'd been exposed to drugs, alcohol, sexual assaults, and old man nudity. Things weren't looking good.

We turned into a small driveway with dirty concrete and a tiny yard.

Marla saw the petrified look on my face. "Tracie," she said apologetically, "I'm sorry, this was the best I could do. Not a lot of people were willing to take in a teenager. Try to adjust, okay? Also, your new foster mom's name is Beth, and she was in a bad car accident a few years ago. Her neck doesn't turn, so try not to stare."

"What do you mean, doesn't turn?"

"You know, like an owl. They can turn their necks to the side, but with her it just stays there. Turned that one way. I just want you to be prepared."

I sighed and nodded. Her neck wasn't what I was worried about.

I grabbed my bags and plodded to the front door. Marla knocked and I held my breath, completely unsure of what was in store for me. Slowly, the door cracked open. The silhouette of a woman, a little taller than me, framed the doorway. A cigarette hung precariously from her mouth. The woman surveyed me, then abruptly told Marla that she was late. She quickly ushered us in.

She didn't look at me. Her face stayed pointed in another direction, and I was glad I had been forewarned. Most of the walls were wood paneling, and the kitchen was a drab yellow, which was made even darker and more uninviting by the gloom. All the curtains were closed. One single light bulb dangled wistfully over a kitchen table. There were dirty dishes in the sink, and the air smelled like a bitter, wet dog.

The woman was wearing an all-black sweat suit and had bowl-cut red hair. Her body was turned to the side so she could stare directly at us. Marla introduced me.

"Thanks for taking me in," I said. I held out my hand. She didn't take it.

"Don't be thinking this is no vacation," she snapped. "I know all about your kind."

She gave me a once-over, like this was a barn sale transaction and asked Marla if I was going to be as much trouble as I was to the last family.

"No, of course she won't," Marla assured her.

"She best not be. You know I don't put up with any sass. I'll send her right back where she came from."

"I've already had a talk with Tracie about her attitude. I don't think you'll have any trouble from her," Marla replied as she placed her hand on my back. She then laid out some paperwork for my new foster mom to sign. Marla flipped each page over quickly.

"Is that all the paperwork? I've got things to do," Beth said.

"Yes, of course. I'll show myself out," Marla said.

She muttered something to me, but I wasn't sure if she was saying bye, or giving me my last rites. As my lower lip started to tremble and an awkward silence took over the room, she waved her hand to me and darted out the door.

I heard the car door slam. I'd been dumped again.

"Did you hear me?"

I turned. "Ma'am?"

"You're going to have to pay attention if you stay here. Come on, girl. Grab your things. Your room is this way."

"Yes, ma'am," I mumbled.

We passed through the living room, where she pointed to a remote control sitting on an end table. "You aren't allowed to touch the remote or watch television, without my permission. Got that?"

"Yes, ma'am."

"Don't touch anything without permission. That goes for food too. Can you remember that?"

"Yes."

"What?"

"Yes, ma'am."

"That's more like it. I won't tolerate bad manners or sass here."

She continued walking and led me down a dark, narrow hallway as I lugged my trash bag. There were no pictures on the walls, not even painted ones of pretend children. She took a left into a small room with twin beds. One side of the room was decorated with posters of teen male celebrities. There was a wooden nightstand between the two beds.

"This'll be where you sleep," she said as she pointed toward the bare-walled side of the room, at a bed with a moth-eaten quilt on top. It was the type of bed you expected to lay on if you murdered someone on the fly and woke up in Angola Prison. My eyes became transfixed on the desk. Someone had obviously dropped off my larger things—computer, television, and bike—before I arrived.

"Your last foster family brought that here yesterday," she said, following my gaze. "Oh, and I know all about you, so don't think you'll be playing games here. You'll be sharing a room with another teenage girl. Her name is Nikki, so you best be getting along. Dinner is at six-sharp. Any questions?"

"No, ma'am."

She slammed the door. I dropped my bag on the floor and folded myself on the Angola bed. Confusion started to set in as I realized Beth hadn't instructed me about what I was to do. Was I supposed to stay in this room until dinner? Springs poked up into my backside. I tried not to move too much, so Beth wouldn't hear. I didn't want to make any more mistakes.

A ripped-out teen magazine picture of River Phoenix stared at me from the opposite wall. He had a giant red heart drawn around his face and slivers of Scotch tape at the top of his head, holding him to the paneling. There was also a picture of Kirk Cameron. He didn't have a heart drawn around him, like River, but I thought he was cuter. I didn't see any pictures of Ricky Schroeder, the only teen star I was interested in. I knew from that one detail that this wasn't going to work out.

The computer reminded me most of home. I didn't even know where home was anymore. Lunchtime came and went, and Beth didn't offer me food or water. That evening, I was still lying on the bed, counting the balls of dust on the ceiling, when I heard a voice at the door.

The door cracked open. I jerked to my feet.

A blonde-haired, brown-eyed girl shuffled in. "You must be the new girl. Hi, I'm Nikki," she said.

"Yes, I'm Tracie," I replied, relieved someone was friendly. Maybe it wouldn't be so bad after all.

We exchanged a few pleasantries, before she said, "I have to go meet a friend down the road to study, but I'll be back later, okay?"

"Sure thing," I said.

I waited on the bed a few more hours, kicking my bag occasionally, to give myself something to do. There was no TV, but there was a small radio on Nikki's side of the room. I chose not to touch it. Amy hadn't liked it when I touched her things.

Finally, there were small whispers at my door.

"No, you open it."

"No, you."

"Okay, we both will at the same time. One, two, three… You were supposed to open at three! Let's do it one more time. One, two, three…"

The door creaked open. Two small heads peeped in. They giggled for a moment, quickly covering their mouths with their tiny hands, then pushed the door a little wider. I hadn't known there were young children in the home. The girl was about seven and wore a thick pair of glasses that were much too large for her head. The boy was eight, only slightly taller, and obviously the one in control.

I smiled to welcome them.

"I'm Garret," he said matter-of-factly. In one breath, he continued, "This is Becky. My mom says you're crazy, and we aren't supposed to talk to you. Do you like kids? We like you. Do you like to play games? Our dog's name is Scrounger, but he's not friendly and—"

Suddenly, the door burst open and hit the wall so hard I thought it might have cracked a hole in it. A tall, gray-haired man with a large build filled the doorway. His face was rough from the sun, his shirt half unbuttoned. Gray chest hair poked out the top of his wife beater underneath. His hands were like leather, and one of them firmly grasped a beer. I assumed this was Charles, my foster dad.

Garret and Becky's eyes grew wide. I closed my eyes and pretended this wasn't happening.

"What are you doing in here?" he roared at the children.

My eyes opened again. "They were just visiting with—"

"Was I talking to you?" he asked, cupping his empty hand to his ear.

"No." I looked back at the floor I'd been staring at for hours.

"'No, sir' is what I should hear. You are going to walk the line here, girl." He took a sip of beer, never taking his eyes off of me. He pulled the can back down from his crusty lips, crinkling the aluminum with his fingers. "You don't even know what you're in for."

"Yes, sir," I mumbled. I'd spent most of my life reading books, pretending I was in them, pretending not to be me. I didn't like to go out and seldom left my room. The longer I sat on the bed, the more confused I got about who I was. I had a sneaking suspicion that Amy had come with my ex-foster parents to drop off the bike and computer. *Why can't I ever get a fresh start?*

Like a human tornado, Charles yanked Garret by the neck and dragged him out. Becky followed with her head hanging low. Moments later, the lash of a belt sounded. Garrett screamed.

"I told both of you that you are never to talk to her, and you are especially never to be alone with her!"

Wop! Wop! Wop!

I put my face in my hands, until Garret's wailing finally stopped. Charles shouted at Becky to go to her room until dinner. I could hear her whimpering through the wall. A few minutes later, Beth came in the room, flinging her hands frantically up in the air.

"Do you see the trouble you caused already? The kids are not to be alone with you. Don't call them in here. Just leave them alone!"

I was terrified of answering back and just nodded. My stomach growled. I hadn't eaten all day, but I wasn't asking for food. I just wanted to crawl under the bed and die a slow, painful death. I was already living the slow and painful part. Death seemed inevitable.

Are most families like this? My memories of Sarah and her family at the ranch were slowly fading. *What is normal? Is there no hope?*

These questions wouldn't be answered.

About an hour later, Nikki came rushing into the room. She threw herself onto the bed and sobbed.

Now what do I do?

"What's wrong? Is it something I did?" I asked, fearing the worst.

"No, no, it's not you," she said, wiping tears onto her sleeve. "Mom just accused me of something. She's so jealous of me and Dad." She went on to explain that "some cute boy" had called and left his number with "Dad," who was half drunk and teasing her about it. "Dad shoved the number into his pocket and when I tried to grab it, Mom grabbed me, pushed me away, and told me to keep my hands off of her husband."

Nikki was devastated, looking to me for answers. I couldn't even answer my own questions yet, much less hers. There seemed to be a very fine line between normal and abnormal, and I kept falling on either side of it.

She explained to me that she had been in foster care most of her life, and this home was one of the better ones she'd been in. *One of the better ones?* She'd been here for over a year now, after passing through about four different homes in the prior several years. Becky, the young girl, was another foster child, but Garret was adopted when he was a baby. They didn't spank the foster children, as it was against policy, but they had other creative ways of punishment. Social Services apparently turned a blind eye because there weren't many foster homes. Garret wasn't a foster child anymore, so he was fair game. He didn't know he was adopted.

"I never did get the boy's number," Nikki finally sobbed, throwing herself into her pillow. "Also," she said, almost as an afterthought, "what did you do to the kids? They said they were both punished because of you."

I DECIDED THAT I was too terrified to eat, so I slipped into bed at seven o'clock. I crawled under the safety of my threadbare quilt, wondering how many other poor souls had slept under it. I ran my hand along its frayed edges. My mom's quilts were much nicer than this.

The doorway darkened with a shadow. "Why didn't you come eat, girl?" Beth asked, standing in the doorway.

"I'm not hungry."

She slammed the door behind her.

I wanted Molly. Needed her. She always made me feel so much better.

The next morning, Beth woke me and told me to get ready for school. "You aren't sleeping all day anymore. Your lounging days are over, girl. I'm on to you," she said. Admittedly, I had taken an almost six-month hiatus from school and was not particularly looking forward to getting back into the routine of studying and homework.

Nikki went to a different school and had already left. I now had makeup and nicer clothes, and I was desperate to get out of this house. Being bullied by people my own age was better than this.

The new school was Ms. LeBlanc's school. As we pulled into the horseshoe drive, I closed my eyes and sighed. Oddly, it felt like I was going backward.

The day went off without a hitch. I didn't make any friends, but I wasn't bullied either. I didn't see Ms. LeBlanc but decided I would look for her once I was settled. The teachers were nice, and I liked them. It was such a huge school that I blended in. No one seemed to notice me. Overall, I enjoyed it and looked forward to going back the next day.

I took the bus home. Once again, I didn't eat and went to bed at seven.

I planned to do the same thing when I got home the next day, but Beth stopped me. "Who do you think you are?"

"Ma'am?"

"You haven't lifted a finger since you've been here. Do you think you're just going to do nothing?"

"Well, no. It's just that I haven't eaten any food. I'm not being any trouble. I've dirtied two glasses, and I don't have much laundry yet, so—"

"So, that's how you get out of work?"

"No, that's not what—"

"You see that pile of laundry on the couch?" She pointed to an entire sofa of laundry, none of which was mine. "Fold it now."

When I was finished folding and sorting it all, I picked up my books and went to my room. A few hours later, Beth appeared.

"I thought I told you to do the laundry."

"I did it. I left it all on the sofa, folded and sorted."

"You calling me a liar?"

I walked with her to the living room. I found laundry scattered everywhere, unfolded. I had heard Garret and Becky playing outside; I knew they couldn't have done this. Nikki was nowhere to be seen. Beth's husband sat in a dark corner in his recliner, sipping rye whiskey from a shot glass and muttering to himself.

"Pick it up and fold it," she hissed.

"I'm not folding it again. Why did you do this?" I couldn't believe what I was seeing. She'd thrown it everywhere.

"You'll do it or be punished."

"I'm not doing it again," I said, pushing past Beth, but before I made it a few steps a strong hand grabbed me by the collar and coiled my arm behind my back. I resisted and struggled like the caged, tormented wild animal I was becoming.

Charles held me tightly, a familiar stink of whiskey and cigarette smoke making me angrier, making me want to fight back. It reminded me of home, the place I left so I wouldn't have to fight ever again.

When we got to the doorway of my bedroom, I tried to go in, but he yanked me by my hair and dragged me further down the hall. At the end of the hall, was a door; he opened it and chucked me inside. "This will teach you to sass back." I heard the unmistakable shifting of a lock.

My pulse raced. I started banging on the door and screaming, "Let me out of here. I can't stand small spaces!"

I banged for a few minutes and then the door opened. A glass of ice water was hurled in.

"Stop banging on the door! This is why no one wants you. Even the crazy house didn't want you!" Beth shouted. Charles stood behind her, glaring at me. The door slammed shut. A lock clicked. I stood, shivering, as streams of water slid down my face. I felt shamed by her words, then intimidated. I wanted to run away again. Then I remembered that no one wanted me.

I pictured my brother bent over his guitar, strumming a few notes, my sister trotting a My Little Pony from one side of the room to the other. I didn't have to envision what my parents were doing. I knew. Mom was reading a book of some sort, possibly a novel set in the 1800s. Dad was either watching television or yelling at someone. I stared into the darkness. Somehow, I felt that I was getting the short end of the stick.

I'd spent so many years of my journey walking toward the light, walking toward a promise, only now to be trapped in darkness. I didn't want to trust adults, anymore, and I wasn't sure if I wanted to be one either. There were many things I'd doubted since I left home, but the one thing I still didn't doubt was that there was a place for me somewhere out there in the world. I just had to find it. At Kate and James's house, heaven had been laid out before me, glistening. Here, I was dammed to hell, to be dragged kicking and screaming into a dark void.

It will be this memory of being wet and locked in a closet that will take me hostage in a nightmare twenty-five years later, causing me to bolt upright in bed. I will grapple with my past. I will remember the things that happened before the closet—being sprayed with water by Kate, smashing an egg on James's bald spot, Molly dancing with me at midnight. When I am an adult and this closet tries to box me in again, these other memories will help set me free.

Chapter 17:

The Mooring Rope

I named the closet she locked me in.
I called it the Dungeon. The next morning, I awoke to another dose of ice water lobbed in my face.

"Rise and shine, princess."

I jerked to my feet. Beth stood in the doorframe.

"You should thank me for letting you sleep in. Now you're running late. Hurry up and get dressed, and this afternoon make sure you come back with a better attitude."

Garret and Becky were arguing over the last Pop-Tart in the kitchen, something I was not allowed to have. "You'll eat the free meals at school," Beth had already informed me, though my bus usually arrived too late for me to eat breakfast.

I looked back at the Dungeon. At some point during the night, someone had tossed a small pillow inside, much like you'd do for a dog.

I trudged to the bathroom. I inspected the reflection in the toothpaste-smudged mirror. I barely recognized myself anymore. The girl in the mirror had sunken eyes from stress and lack of nourishment. She was pale with matted hair because of falling asleep with her wet head leaning against a wall.

For years, I had wanted to wear makeup, to be like everyone else. Now, mascara ran down my face. I looked deep into my green eyes and saw the vast emptiness in them. They had sparkled like emeralds, just a few months earlier. I had laughed and been proud of myself. I had fallen in love with Kate and James's children, had fallen in love with Kate and James. I wanted the girl in the mirror to save me, but she herself needed to be saved.

"Tracie, hurry up," Beth hollered. "Stop playing around or I won't let you sleep late anymore."

I wiped the black maze of mascara from my face, fetched my books, and ran to catch my bus, still wearing the same clothes I'd had on the day before.

That afternoon when I came home, the same pile of laundry was waiting for me, along with another load that needed to be ironed and hung. Beth stood near it, ready to pounce on me. I immediately picked up everything, folded and ironed everyone's clothes, and this time put them away in everyone's rooms, except for Beth's room. She had told me not to enter her room.

At dinnertime, Beth came to fetch me.

"I'm not hungry," I said quietly, even though my stomach felt like an empty pit.

"Then you need to come clean the kitchen when we're finished."

"I'm not eating and I'm tired," I countered, completely drained. "Can't Nikki do them?"

"You live here. You will work." She marched off, muttering about how lazy I was.

When everyone was finished eating, she hollered for me to go clean. The number of dishes left on the table, piled in the sink, and on the countertops was dumbfounding. The rice cooker was still full of rice and beamed an orange light at me. A large greasy pot with brown roux, streaming down its sides, a pot with some corn left in it, and a pot with some beans left in it sat on the stove. Roux slid down the oven door and onto the floor. The dog was furiously lapping it up. The morning breakfast pots, pans, and dishes were still in the sink.

I wanted to cry so badly, but I was too tired and didn't want to spend another night in the closet. I realized that, by being in foster care, I had traded bondage for slavery and might never, ever taste freedom.

"When you're finished," she said, "there are some towels to fold."

I didn't even look at her. "Yes, ma'am."

While I washed the dishes, I gazed out of the kitchen window into the disappearing light. The yard was barely visible, hidden by a thin tree that had no beauty. The rest of the world was hidden from my view as well. I felt I would forever be someone's maid.

After I cleaned the plates and the glasses, I scrubbed the pots and pans. Becky walked in and put an empty glass on the countertop. I smiled at her and she stood there for a second, as if wanting to say something.

"Becky!" Beth shouted, and she quickly scampered away.

Just as I was finished in the kitchen, the phone rang. Beth answered it and said, "Who is this?" There was a moment's silence. "Okay, she can speak."

I was completely surprised someone was calling me. I hoped it was Kate, telling me that Amy had been a terrible mistake, that she was sorry and would never send me away again.

Beth tossed me the phone. "It's the nuthouse."

"Hello?" I said, nervously twirling the spiral cord with my fingers.

"Hello, Tracie." It was Molly! She asked me how I was adjusting.

"Oh, I'm doing great," I lied. Beth hovered, just inches away. She leaned in closer to listen, trying to intercept any secret signals I might send over the phone.

"I found you a church to attend. I've already talked to the pastor, and I talked to Social Services, and it is within your right to attend any church you want to. No one can tell you any different."

Beth, whose ear was pressed against the receiver, frowned. She started wildly gesturing for me to hang up.

I told Molly that it was great to hear from her, and I would write to her soon.

"You'll be going to *our* church on Sunday," Beth snapped as soon as I hung up.

"No. Molly said I can go to any church I want to, and y'all have to make the arrangements. Besides, it's not far from here." I couldn't help grinning. She wasn't getting any "helping that poor demented foster child" brownie points off me at her church.

"Finish cleaning the kitchen, and when you're finished fold those towels," she snapped. "Also, you won't be allowed to talk to that woman anymore."

I didn't care about the towels. I would have folded the laundry for the entire world that night. I had heard from Molly, and she was setting me up for success.

Maybe things will get better.

My second week at Beth's, I still hadn't eaten any meals in her home, only at school. Beth scoffed every time I walked by her in the evenings, said I was worthless, and, after I did the laundry, didn't want to see me. I didn't know if I was worthless or not, but I started stuffing papers in the soles of my shoes again. I was desperate and hoped that God would provide a way out, something better.

The next evening, when Beth and I returned from one of her appointments—she didn't trust me to be left alone in the house—Nikki and the two children were back from school. As we reached the front door, she glared at me. "Do I have to do everything? Open the door for me. Show some manners, girl." Beth rarely addressed me by name, preferring instead to use a drawn-out and dramatically pronounced *gurrrl*. She had nothing in her hands, but I pulled the door open for her. It occurred to me that I was officially her live-in maid.

That weekend, I discovered that they had an older married daughter when we went to her house to eat lunch on Saturday. Nikki didn't come; she was at a friend's house. I strongly suspected the friend was a boy. Meanwhile, Beth didn't even allow me outside by myself.

On the way, we passed down roads that were vaguely familiar of when I lived in this town with my parents. We passed a dirty quarter horse on a small muddy lot. It had been years since I'd seen a horse, and it reminded me of the beautiful palomino Goldie that I used to ride on the ranch with Sarah. I smiled as I remembered how I was secretly part of the rich, once.

As the car crawled by, I wondered how many people passed this horse every day and didn't care about its condition, which was deplorable. Hundreds of cars passed each day, and everyone just stared vacantly ahead, distracted by their own lives, pretending that this giant, once beautiful animal wasn't standing helplessly in the mud. It was probably too much trouble to get involved.

Beth and Charles's daughter lived in a cinder block home. When we got out, Garrett ran to the front door just as it opened. A tall redhead stepped out. She looked about twenty-five. He gave her a hug and went inside like this was his second home. I was not introduced to her. I was sure she'd already been told about me, the lazy *gurrl*. I settled onto a corner of the couch and stared at the floor. Beth and her daughter stayed in the kitchen, cooking, laughing, and telling stories. On a few occasions, their voices lowered to whispers. Charles and his son-in-law sprawled out in the living room, drinking from beer cans stuffed in koozies. I asked if I could go outside.

"No."

Becky and Garret were playing outside, so I supposed Beth figured I might cause them harm, somehow. I had started putting papers in my shoes again, a last-ditch effort for hope. I could feel them in that moment, and it reinforced my faith once more.

I want to be somewhere that feels like a home. I wasn't sure how much longer I wanted to wait. The thought occurred to me that I could run away again.

Lunch was baked ham with pineapple rings, homemade macaroni and cheese, green bean casserole, and peach cobbler for dessert. I was so hungry that my stomach was knotting up. When Beth said we could eat, I tried not to rush into the kitchen too fast. I scooped up as much as I could on my plate, trying my best not to look greedy. The smell was intoxicating. I closed my eyes and inhaled. It had been over half a year since I'd eaten a home-cooked meal.

There were only six chairs at the table, four for the adults and two for Becky and Garret. Beth told me this when she saw me walking toward a chair. She pointed to a spot on the floor near a litter box, out of everyone's way, in case someone wanted to get up for seconds. I asked if I could sit on the sofa in the living room if I was careful not to spill.

"This is exactly what I'm talking about." Beth rolled her eyes to her daughter, who had already started wiggling her finger and shaking her head. I wasn't going to eat in her fancy cinder block living room. "She just doesn't listen. Always has to have things her way."

She told me to sit on the floor and be grateful that someone had labored to prepare a nice meal for me. I felt tears of humiliation rush to my eyes. The floor was cold and hard, and the litter box smelled. I sneezed. Beth said, "Leave it to Tracie to get everyone sick."

My cheesy macaroni began to smell like cheesy cat poo, so I tried to eat it before it tasted like poo too. The cat then decided the time was just right to do his business. Becky noticed the glorious event and put her hand over her mouth to suppress a giggle, which only drew everyone's attention. My face turned red as everyone started laughing. I decided I wasn't hungry anymore and stood to put my plate near the sink. Among the snickers, Beth proclaimed, "It's just like Tracie to waste food we've worked so hard to prepare." She looked at me sternly. "Don't expect anything else today. You aren't going to be wasteful and ungrateful."

Still hungry, I trudged back to the living room.

"Tracie, you're full of cat hair now. Don't sit on the furniture." Beth pointed at the floor near the litter box again.

I looked over at the couch, which was finely coated in cat hair, then back to Beth. "I'll just stand."

She shot daggers at me with her eyes as I stood near the litter box. I watched the macaroni disappear and wished I'd finished mine. My plate still sat on the counter, but I was afraid to touch it. After they were all finished, her daughter fetched some dirty plates from the table and started to clean the kitchen.

"Oh, no." Beth rubbed the small of her back, lovingly. "Let Tracie take care of this while we visit in the living room. She needs to learn not to be so ungrateful."

Her daughter was hesitant, and I quietly hoped she'd be in my corner on this. But she put the plates down and walked into the living room with everyone else. Once I was alone, I secretly speared a leftover pineapple ring from someone's plate and greedily devoured it.

On the way home, I sat next to the window, waiting to pass by the horse, anxious to remember my days as a friend of Sarah. I was pretending now that I was back in the station wagon at her side. Instead of seeing a cluster of mobile homes and collapsing houses, I imagined rolling hills, daisies, a whitewashed fence lining the road, and quarter horses racing alongside the car. We passed the horse in the mud, and I stared at it, my heart sad. It deserved to be taken care of.

Beth was busy in the front seat, murmuring about how I'd tried so vehemently to ruin the day for her. "Did you see her look at me when I told her to sit on the floor? She wanted to say something but knew better, and she can thank her lucky stars for that. Who knows what thoughts go on in her head? She is of the devil with those monster-green eyes. That's a bad seed, that one."

Charles vacantly stared down the long road ahead, never answering.

This was not what I'd bargained for when I had originally set out for California.

Back at the house, I slipped into the backyard to see what it had to offer. Beth followed me outside. "What are you up to?"

"I just want some air."

"There's air in the house. You had better not be up to anything."

A puppy yelped in pain where the yard bordered the neighbors. There was a chain-link fence separating us and a wire running along the bottom, leaving a small gap between the ground and the fence. The puppy's head was stuck underneath the wire, and he was wailing.

"Really, Tracie," Beth huffed. "Don't just stand there. Go pull the wire off its neck, so it'll stop screaming."

I sprinted to the yelping animal, wondering why it was panicking. There seemed to be plenty of room for him to pull his body out without choking.

When I got closer, I noticed he looked like a Golden Retriever puppy. I reached down to pull the wire up, so he could crawl back into his own yard. As I grabbed the wire with both hands, volts of electricity surged through my body. The dog didn't move. Still holding on, I tried to push him out of the way with my foot, but he panicked and flopped back.

I let go of the wire with one hand so I could yank the puppy to freedom with the other. My hands still stinging, I picked him up to hold and comfort him, but the neighbor rushed out her back door and said, "Oh, that's my puppy."

I handed it to her over the fence and turned to look at Beth. She was smiling to herself, not a warm smile, but a manic smile that seemed to be just for herself. She uncrossed her arms and motioned for me to go back into the house. I went straight to the bathroom and ran cool water over my red hands. Later, when Nikki returned, I told her about what had happened. I showed her the red line that had burned into both of my palms.

"Oh, that's an electric wire they installed to keep possums and raccoons out of the yard. You should have known better than to touch it."

I didn't tell her that Beth had told me to. I would have helped the puppy, anyway, but would've used a stick instead of my hands. Still, I trusted Beth even less after that incident.

I told Charles what time I needed to go to church the next morning, since Beth couldn't drive because of her injury. She looked at me and said, "You know you're ruining our weekend. Now my daughter has to bring us home. Charles has to stay home and wait around for you. We can't go to church as a family. No wonder your last foster family got rid of you."

Molly must have already called and told the church about me, because the next morning, two men greeted me at the entrance and sat me beside a nice elderly couple. After service, the pastor walked with me to the car and stopped to talk to Charles about attending church with me the next Sunday. I climbed into the passenger seat as Charles shot me an evil side glare. The smell of whiskey wafted through the car's interior. Charles bit on his lower lip but impassively listened to the pastor rattle on that he was welcome to come in with me on Sundays if he liked.

I already had figured out that Charles hated church and suspected that words were building up inside of him. He revved up the engine for a moment, before letting it idle back down. The pastor grasped his Bible, firmly, as Charles reached under his seat and pulled out a little paper bag with a whiskey bottle tucked inside. With the engine still idling, he shifted the car in reverse, held up the bottle, and grinned, "I already know I'm going to hell. I'll be damned if I'm going to feel guilty about it."

———

AS SOON AS I stepped foot inside the house, Beth handed me a toilet brush and barked that since I liked to ruin everyone's Sunday, it was time for me to clean. Moments later, she pressed a list of chores in my hand. I appraised the list: scrub the toilets, hand wash the baseboards, sweep, mop, dust, vacuum, laundry, and cut the grass. As I scrubbed the stained porcelain, I imagined what my father was probably doing: laid back on a large oak chair in the kitchen reading a newspaper, waiting for Mom to serve him lunch—the same thing he'd done for hundreds of Sundays. His life, unlike mine, had chugged on, unhampered. In contrast, my world had wobbled off its axis. All I could think of was that Dad did the crime and the only one who seemed to be doing the time was me. I was hushed by the world, cast in homes of strangers who felt nothing for me, to live in shame, while he continued to hunt, fish, and watch Sunday reruns of *Kung Fu*.

Beth made me her personal obsession. In my months in foster care, I'd learned there was no pity for foster children, as if being abused or neglected by one's parents is some sort of penance for past sins. I wasn't sure what Beth did all day, but there was always a good deal of work waiting for me, almost as if she had purposefully created it. I wondered who was wearing all those clothes.

Since I didn't go to school on the weekends, I ate what Beth cooked, which was usually just a slab of flavorless meat that tasted like cardboard and maybe some runny potatoes and beans. But I was usually ravenous by the time Saturday rolled around and would eat whatever she put on the table.

One evening, Beth turned her chair so she could face me, her steely-eyed glare watching me eat. "Who taught you how to cut meat?"

"No one," I said as I tried to saw through the tough meat.

"Well, that's obvious. Becky and Garret do a better job at cutting food than you do. Lazy people don't know how to cut meat."

"I'm not lazy," I replied as I shoveled a spoonful of beans in my mouth.

"Lazy and sassy. You sassed your last foster parents, but you won't sass me. I'll tell you that." She looked around to make sure everyone was as uncomfortable as I was. The table was silent, except for the sounds of knives sawing through meat.

"I didn't sass them," I said.

I picked up the pepper shaker to try to improve the meat, but the pepper wouldn't come out. I unscrewed the lid to check for something lodged in the cap. Beth snapped it from my hand and dumped the entire jar on my food.

"You don't like the meal I prepared for you, princess?" Beth said, getting louder. "You want some pepper? Is this enough?"

I studied the mountain of pepper on my plate and said nothing.

"Well, is it?" she shouted as she yanked my shirt.

My head bobbed as the yanking continued.

Charles slammed down his fork, making all the glasses quiver. "Why don't you leave her alone and let her eat? I would like to have some peace at the table."

"Oh, you want peace? Well, then you will get it!" she hollered back.

Beth jerked me away from my half-eaten meal. "What are you doing?" I asked, but I already knew where we were headed. To the Dungeon.

I'd long learned it did no good to bang on the door. She would eventually come to get me out to clean the kitchen. An hour later, the door creaked open.

"You thought you were going to get out of work, didn't you, princess?" Beth asked.

I shook my head and proceeded to follow her into the kitchen, but she stopped in the living room and settled into a lecture about how I needed to go to confession so I wouldn't spend too much time in purgatory. I quietly stood with my arms crossed as she droned on and on about how the Southern Baptists were teaching me to be rebellious and lazy.

"I think you should go to our church. It would be best for all of us. Do you honestly think I'm going to sit back and let someone living under my roof get brainwashed by the Baptists?"

"I'm not being brainwashed," I answered.

Beth's mouth dropped a good half inch, and a blast of hot air rushed in my direction.

"Are you talking back to me? Is this what the Baptists are teaching you? To disrespect your elders?"

She stood erect and tried to position herself tall to show dominance over me. I tried to stand taller.

She yanked some rosary beads from around a little statue on a shelf.

"I am going to learn you some prayers tonight while there is still some hope for you," she said trying to press the beads in my hand.

"No," I said and placed my hands behind my back.

"Girl, you better take these beads. You aren't going to break up this family, sitting in a separate church every week."

Charles let out a low grunt from a dimly lit corner of the room, unscrewed a whiskey cap, and downed a quick shot.

"What you really need is an exorcism," she continued.

I stood, frozen with my hands behind my back. I felt like I couldn't let her win this. It seemed to be the one battle I needed to win.

Beth narrowed her eyes and stood inches from me; her hands fisted tightly around the rosary beads. She stared into my face waiting for me to break down and give her the Hail Mary she so desperately wanted.

I didn't.

I SUSPECTED BETH had other issues that it supported her in her brutal treatment of me. Sometimes her eyes rolled back into her head, and she hesitated slightly before she spoke.

She was always, always angry. If there was an evening with no laundry, she followed me to my room, sharing her thoughts of me. "It must be nice to come from a rich family and try to glide your way through foster care like a princess. You think that you're going to lie around all day, just reading those books of yours? Well, you have another thing coming, girl."

She went on to say that I thought I was special because I came from a rich family, which she inferred because I had a handful of nice clothes due to Kate's good taste.

Once in my room, I was not allowed to close my door, lest I try to secretly chisel an escape hole. I had to be always accessible to her, to be seen when she walked down the hallway. I could see where she was making efforts to go through my journal, so sometimes I wrote things about her for her to read. I carefully placed the journal, so I would know at the end of the day if she'd picked it up. It was always moved.

I need another Molly.

It was driving me crazy that I no longer had freedom. My entire life had been about hoping for this and hoping for that. Fear kept me shackled. I just wanted to be set free. I was nothing and I had nothing, but I kept my hopes in my soles. The little slivers of hope were my freedom and were always just out of my reach.

I felt anchored down by foster care, hooked to a world that punished me for wanting to be free. A world that pushed me through cycles of torment and abuse, that gave and took away, that plotted a mooring scheme for my life. When I didn't do the dance that was expected of me, the mooring rope tethering me to this new world was shortened. Knotted. No one seemed satisfied at how taut the rope became, no matter how closely it came to resemble a short, thickly braided noose. I struggled to loosen myself from it, but I seemed bound to it. The more I struggled, the more it suffocated me.

———

ABOUT A WEEK LATER, when I came home from school and walked into my room, Beth was sitting on my bed, holding my journals. "I saw what you wrote about me."

"And?"

"And you are no longer allowed to write."

"You can't stop me from writing."

"You are living under my roof."

"I don't want to live under *your* roof. I hate it here."

"I took you in. Be grateful, girl."

"I'm your personal slave. I clean your whole house while you do nothing. You lock me in a closet and throw water on me. I want out of here. Call my worker!"

"No."

"I want to talk to her about you and how evil you are."

Beth's eyes blazed as she pursed her lips. "No."

I tossed my books on the floor and fled on my bike.

I biked a few miles toward the center of town and imagined myself homeless, living under a bridge. I passed an older lady getting into her car. I spun the bike around and lurched toward her.

"Excuse me, can I use your phone?" I hollered.

She appraised me. "What for, dear?"

"I need to call the police on my foster parents. They've been abusing me."

"Put your bike over there," she said immediately, motioning toward her house. "The police station isn't far. I'll drop you off." I parked my bike and hopped into her car. My entire body was shaking. She patted me on the leg and smiled. I knew there was kindness in the world and, sometimes, I got little spurts of it. Just enough to keep me going.

She pulled into the station, walked me in, and helped arrange for someone to talk to me. I was familiar with this station. This was where I was brought the first time I ran away. An officer peered out of an office and motioned for me. I thanked the lady for her kindness and walked into the office.

He picked up the phone to call my worker. "Are we going to make this a routine, you running away?" he asked. I said nothing.

When Marla was finally on the phone, he handed me the receiver. She'd already talked to Beth and received her version of the story. "You have to go back, Tracie," she said.

"Oh, no, I'm not."

"I have nowhere for you to go."

"They locked me in a closet."

"She said they put you on time-out."

"Then why did a door lock? Why was water thrown on me? Why a closet?"

"She never locked the door, and you knocked a glass of water out of her hand."

"You believe that? Why would she be sipping a tall glass of ice water by a closet?"

"Should I believe you?"

"Yes!"

"I have no place for you to go, Tracie."

"Your house?"

"No, I'm not approved to take in kids."

"Get approved."

"You have to go back. You don't understand. I have no homes that will take in teenagers, especially runaways."

"What about the people who took in the two small kids from Kate and James, the ones I used to live with?"

"They don't take in teenagers."

"Can you ask them?"

"I will."

"Ask now."

There was a long, muffled silence, then she said, "Okay, I'll call you back."

My fingers tapped nervously as I waited for her to call back. When she finally did, I asked, "Well?"

"They said yes."

My heart beat fast, and I felt a great rush of relief. This was my ticket.

"Come get me."

"They aren't ready right now. It's getting late. I'll pick you up tomorrow morning first thing. Don't go to school."

After a lengthy discussion, I finally agreed.

I was now suspicious of every adult who walked into my life. Each adult I'd encountered had shaped me, made me more cynical.

When Charles finally walked in the station, he stared hard at me and said nothing. I humbly followed him to his car. It was the longest ride of my life.

Beth furiously tossed things around the house all evening, but she didn't ask me to clean anything. No food was offered. I told Nikki goodbye, that I was leaving, but there was no emotional parting. She hadn't been around much.

I was too excited to sleep, and the clock seemed to tick slower than usual. This was my last night on the Angola bed. I smiled from ear to ear at the little sliver of moonlight peeking through the window. *I think I'm going to make it after all.*

CHAPTER 18:

FRONTIER

I was ready and waiting for Marla the next morning. When I heard her voice, I rushed past her and Beth with my trash bag full of clothes into the waiting car. Someone would come back for the rest of my things. When Marla got in, she said, "You better make this next one work."

I tried to explain that it wasn't my fault, but she didn't want to hear any of it. We drove for about fifteen minutes before we turned down an unpaved road. Old men with gray beards glanced up at us as they tilled their gardens or fed their dogs. Women rocking on their front porches watched impassively as we crawled by, sometimes waving.

"Is that it?" I asked each time we approached a home.

"No, that's not it."

Soon, houses started disappearing until there was nothing but cows grazing in dull patchwork fields. I glanced in the side mirror as a plume of fine dust rose.

By the time we pulled over some raised railroad tracks, the entire car was coated in dust, and as we made our final curve, I peered out of the grimy windshield. My eyebrows lifted slightly. I was about to start my new life as a pioneer, apparently. A real-life *Little House on the Prairie*, Laura Ingalls Wilder, go-make-your-own-soap-while-Pa is-out-shooting-supper-in-the-woods, play-the-fiddle-for-evening-entertainment, pioneer.

My new foster home was a modest clapboard house with a rusty tin roof. It was surrounded by hundreds of acres of straw-like pastureland. There was an addition on the side that I would later find out was the master bedroom and master bath. A leaning, two-story cypress barn was about a hundred feet behind the back of the house. There were lots of chickens, dozens of them, and they seemed to have free range of the yard. They started running for their lives when they saw us pulling up.

My new foster mom, April, waved at us. Her hair was long, straight, and sun-bleached. Jen ran straight to me. I reached down to hug her and realized just how much I missed my own sister. I walked with Jen up to the front porch.

"Welcome to our home," April said. "It isn't much, but we like it."

"Oh, it's great," I replied.

She asked how I'd been doing and if I liked the country. After just two minutes, I was pretty sure that April, unlike my last foster mom, would not encourage me to grab a live electric fence or hurl ice water at me.

April invited us inside. There was a hand-stitched piece of artwork framed in the foyer that had the words "Build Your House on a Rock" awkwardly embroidered underneath. The walls throughout the home were garnished with stitched maxims, mostly Bible sayings. I noticed right away there was only a tiny black-and-white television.

Marla left after she had all her necessary paperwork signed, and April asked if I was hungry or needed anything. I told her I was a bit hungry, as I hadn't eaten that morning or the evening before. She flew to the kitchen and moments later a cheese sandwich materialized. Jen kept running back and forth to her room, to show me the different toys she'd accumulated since the last time I saw her.

April's husband, Raymond, arrived soon and told me he was happy I would be staying with them. Then he announced to April that he'd lost his job that morning. April sucked on her cheeks. Raymond said that it wasn't a problem since he was meant to live off the land anyway. They had plenty of chickens, fruit trees, and free government cheese.

Later that afternoon, their children and Michael walked in from school. Connie was the oldest daughter, fourteen. Her eyes were deep blue and mesmerizing. Jake looked just like his father, and at thirteen he towered over me. Josh was eleven, Fred was nine, and Kayla was seven and the youngest of their biological children. I couldn't make up my mind as to what color her hair was, but I found out that she liked to spy and tattle. Connie had nicknamed her "Big Mouth." When Michael saw me, he ran straight for me with his arms stretched out, and I knew that this would be my last foster home.

―

AT FIRST, LIVING OUT in the middle of nowhere seemed like a great adventure. Connie and I would take long walks and sometimes picked giant buckets of berries that April made into jam or pies. However, living so far out meant that we couldn't go anywhere, like the movies or participate in any activity that required a vehicle to get there. There was no gas money or movie money, so we had to entertain ourselves by singing or walking through the blossoming fields of alfalfa.

There was that old black-and-white television in the house, but we weren't allowed to watch it. It sat on its brown stand for emergency purposes, but it never got turned on. I had a nice color one I used as my computer monitor that I kept in the bedroom I shared with the other girls, and sometimes, with the help of a lookout, we pulled up the antennas and snuck a show or two. We got caught once when our lookout wasn't paying attention. Raymond shouted and everyone scattered like roaches. We all got double chores as punishment and didn't do it again.

The simple things in life, I'd sometimes taken for granted, weren't so simple anymore. The toilet barely flushed, so we used a bucket for our tissue. The bathroom window stayed open most of the time. The view from the toilet was scenic though. Outside, the fields resembled a brown patchwork quilt, spread out before you while you did your business.

April was always canning, freezing, and pickling different fruits and vegetables from the trees and garden that we all tended to. Once or twice a week, she baked a fresh loaf of bread. Life was different but not unbearable.

We got watery milk, plastic cheese, and cereal that tasted like squares of hay once a month from a government building. We were only allowed milk if we were having cornbread and sugar for supper, or for the square cereal. Each of us received one ounce to pour over our bread and sugar to try to make it soggy.

April made everyone's clothes, by either recycling clothing or using old materials that I knew Amy wouldn't be caught dead wearing. In the early morning, before school, Connie and I hung clothes on two long wires stretched across the yard. We refused to touch the boys' underwear, so we used a long stick to position them on the wire.

We all pulled our weight, equally. I never had to open any doors for anyone. Sometimes the boys cleaned the kitchen and sometimes the girls fed the chickens. Connie and I were happy not mingling with the poultry and livestock, so we had no problem volunteering in the kitchen.

I was living poor, but happy. I didn't have to worry about being forced to go out, because we couldn't afford for me to. Since there was no money for entertainment, Connie and I climbed a rickety ladder, leading up to a hayloft in the barn to hide away from the boys, and we secretly sang and danced up there. We laughed until we cried, and never cried for any other reason. Between songs, I told Connie that I wasn't classy enough to live at my last two foster homes.

"I think this is where I was meant to be," I said.

"Do you mean at our house?" She laughed. "Or the barn?"

I had to think about it a second, before replying. "The barn."

———

COYOTOES HOWLED NIGHTLY, whether at the moon or at us, I didn't know. Sometimes they sounded unusually close, and the next morning, chickens would be missing. The master bedroom and master bath addition were the only rooms in the house with a small window air conditioning unit and heater. At night, they closed their bedroom door so the heat and air conditioning couldn't escape. They also had their own hot water tank but could only afford to heat the one tank.

Two or three times a week, we filed into the big blue van to go to church. All the seats in the back of the van had been removed and replaced with benches to accommodate eight passengers. The road was long and full of potholes, so eventually I learned to automatically dig my nails into the bench before we hit one. Since the ride was long, we sang all the way there and back.

Even with all the struggles, I was comfortable. There was a stark difference between struggling and being abused. We were struggling. They were strict, but not abusive, like Beth or my dad.

It was a hard winter, so cold, that I went weeks without taking a bath. The hot water tank was turned down so low, I thought ice cubes would come out of the spigot. Whenever my skin started to feel tacky enough, I'd sponge myself off in the bathroom and wash my hair in the sink. We slept with as many clothes and blankets on as we could. Sometimes, the two younger girls crawled out of their beds and slept in between Connie and me for the extra warmth. It reminded me of the Christmas when I rode in the back of my dad's pickup truck.

———

I WAS BACK TO seeing my parents every other week. My father, tired of explaining to people why I was away, and tired of paying a large child support payment to Social Services every month, offered me a car to come back home. I declined. One sweltering summer day, April and I were perched on wooden chairs on the back porch, while the others picked berries. The fields around the home were rolling and lush; the air smelled of jasmine and oak.

"What are you thinking about?" April asked.

"I'm thinking it's time to put my past behind me, but I don't know how. It feels like it's weighing me down. I don't know how to move forward. I feel stuck in a rut, like there's more to me than this. Does that make any sense? I wish I could just bury the old me and start over."

April studied me. "Go get your journals."

Part of me didn't want to, but another part of me was curious.

When I came back toting the journals under my arm, she was standing with my shovel—the one meant for digging holes or hitting serial killers. She extended it toward me. "You once told me that you write when you're angry and that your past hurts you. All of that is in those journals. It's time to let go, but it must be your decision. You can bury them in a back field or behind the barn, whichever you choose, and then walk away, or you can carry them around forever."

I smiled indecisively as I took the shovel. As I made my way into the field, I got excited. Initially, I headed for the barn, but as I got closer, I wasn't so sure my past belonged there. I looked toward an old oak tree, standing upright and tall like a sentry, its lower limbs resting lazily down on the ground. Spanish moss hung, like wisps of an old wise man's beard.

Sometimes Connie and I sat on the limbs and laughed and talked. Other times, I lay under it, and the shade protected me from the sun as I stared into the deep blue sky. The tree was an old friend, sandwiched between the house and the railroad track we sometimes walked on.

In the end, I decided to entrust the tree with guardianship of my secrets, and among its roots was where I buried my past. Everything I'd written, thought, or cried about would be buried there. As I stood under it, I knew the ghosts of my past could no longer haunt me. They would stay there forever, and I could move forward.

I dug a deep, narrow hole under the tree and dropped my journals in it, then took one last look. They held the last few years of thoughts and emotions that had once kept me composed, but now kept me shackled to my old life. I pushed dirt over them, until the hole was filled, then slipped into the barn and dropped the shovel in a barrel with other farm tools. In the moment, it seemed so very insignificant, and yet, like my first steps on the railroad tracks, parting ways with this shovel was everything. When I emerged from the barn, I felt like the weight of the world was off my shoulders.

THERE WERE SIX OF us picking berries together on either side of the railroad track. I decided to find a fresh spot, off to myself, and started walking. The trees were thick with leaves and brush, but through it all I could make out the modest house that had been my home, for about a year now. Then something else caught my eye.

It looked like a deer near a patch of lush grass. I continued toward it, my hand just over my eyes to block the sun, the tarnished rails at my side. As I neared the patch, I tripped and fell, small rocks stabbed lightly into my palms, my small sack of berries spilling.

The deer scampered away, but I didn't get up immediately. I leaned against the track and wrapped my arms around my legs. A gust of wind pushed my frizzy hair off the edges of my face, and I continued to squint into the light.

I investigated the distance, the miles upon miles of tarnished track and realized that this was the same track I walked so long ago. It ran straight toward the little town I ran away from almost two years earlier.

Eventually, if I had kept walking instead of asking for help from Ms. LeBlanc, I would have passed this spot. Had I kept walking that day, I would've seen the little white house, sitting in the middle of nowhere. I would've stood in this same spot in the sun, scoping out the place. I maybe even would have ventured a little closer and asked for a drink of water.

Now, here I was, perched on the same track, slowly rocking back and forth. Over the last two years, I'd emerged from my cocoon as a new person. And wasn't that what I wanted for myself?

I felt like a butterfly, flying whichever way the wind blew. No matter what direction I went in, my subtle decisions had monumental effects on the lives of others and myself. What would have happened if I had made it to California? Eventually, everything comes full circle, and then the wind blows again.

The other kids were hurriedly filling their buckets and bags with berries. No one seemed to notice I had slipped away. My eyes followed the stretch of track beside them, the track that led to Texas and eventually to California. The path I never took. I'd been in foster care for close to two years. Age out. Age out. Age out. The words tumbled around in my head. They made me cringe. I hated them the moment I first heard them and still did.

As I stared into the bleak distance that led back to the home where my parents lived, I pondered my situation. The family I was living with was nice to me, and they were good people. I missed hot baths though. I missed Gabby and Bubba. I missed food that didn't have free-range chicken in it. When I turned eighteen, I'd have nowhere to go. April had already told me that I couldn't drive their vehicles, and we lived fifteen miles from the nearest store, so I couldn't even get a job to save money. She had also mentioned, on a few occasions, that I needed to be thinking about my future. It had made me uncomfortable that she brought it up because I wasn't green anymore. I knew things now. The money stopped at eighteen, and so would my time in the modest farmhouse.

I could fill my backpack with water, clothing, and pie, start walking again—and if I aged out, this is what I would do. I believed that I could make it to California, though I no longer had a plan, and no longer would anyone care, because I would be an adult. People cared more about children. The younger you were, the more they cared.

Before I left home, I had only spoken to a handful of people my entire life. I dwelled quietly in my own solidarity, hoping to make it to the age of eighteen. I had never caused any trouble and had stayed on the honor roll, until I just couldn't give anymore. Since I left home, I had been chased through a forest by strange men, gotten locked up, been groped by both men and women, been humiliated, pushed, shoved, beaten, fallen hungry, and I may or may not have eaten cat hair.

After several minutes of sitting deep in thought, I stared back across that track and realized that my younger brother had a job, my sister got anything she wanted, and I was the one sitting on a bed of rocks in the middle of nowhere. I wasn't even sure what lessons I'd learned, if any. My parents weren't the best parents, and I didn't want to go back, but the people I was living with could barely support me. The fear of living on my own, under a bridge, rattled me.

I stood on top of the rail and rocked back and forth. The papers were still in my soles, different hopes and dreams on a different part of the rail. I imagined how humiliating it would be to go crawling back home, imagined myself apologizing. I pictured Dad puffing on a cigarette, telling the neighbors I was nothing but a liar who'd crawled back home, only after I'd seen the error of my ways.

I had tried to slingshot myself to the moon. It had, without a doubt, been in my crosshairs as I chucked myself into the universe. But along the way, a cable had snapped, and I'd sailed right past the giant orb of normalcy and floated into the stale darkness. Now, I prepared for the free fall back to reality. No one had told me what to do if I missed my mark, if I failed.

Maybe I was ready to concede to fatalism. I couldn't live off other people for the rest of my life. There was a steady *tick-tick* in the back of my head, counting down the seconds, reminding me that time was running out. I'd age out of foster care, and someday I'd be homeless.

I didn't want to still be wearing this same pair of shoes in ten years, with gray tape holding them together. Before I finished rocking on the rails, before I stepped off, I knew that I had long been tired of playing Laura Ingalls Wilder. It was fun at first, but the frontier life wasn't for me. I looked up at the sky and closed my eyes, letting out a deep sigh.

It was time to go home.

PART THREE

Chapter 19:

The Circus

It was the only place I'd ever known, and despite all its chaos, misery, and drama, it was the only place I felt I belonged. It had been almost two years since I'd uprooted myself. I realized that my struggle was what made me who I was, that I would continue to grow and thrive and be myself, but life would still be hard. Some people were meant to have easy lives. I just wasn't one of them.

I called my social worker and told her that I would like to return home. She started up the process with no questions asked. I had admitted defeat, accepted it. I was young, and I was weak. Too young to be so tired. Going home was not what I wanted to do, but it was what I had to do. Defeat was hard. Conceding to the person who defeated me was harder.

As part of Social Service's plan to transition me back home, I was to speak to my parents on the phone a few times. One day, I called, and Dad answered. He was the only person home. We spoke for a few minutes, and as I was about to hang up his voice softened, as if he was talking to a small child. He said that there was something he needed to talk to me about, privately. He muttered inaudibly, then I heard the words, "…made so many mistakes, it's past due." He told me that he loved me, and we hung up. I stood holding the receiver in my hand, long after the line disconnected. What he said and the tone he said it in—the awkwardness of it—made me wonder if he wanted to apologize. It felt like he did. When the dial tone sounded, I snapped out of my trance. *Maybe there is hope for my dad, after all.*

More than thirty years later, I'm still waiting to hear what he wanted to tell me.

On the day I was to return home, I packed my trash bags for the final stretch of my childhood journey, right back where I started from. April walked in and told me that my social worker had arrived. I thanked her for taking me in when no one else would.

"We've enjoyed having you," she said. "I hope you get wherever it is you want to go."

I gave her a quick embrace, then lugged my bags to the car.

Marla was at the wheel once more. The road we traveled ran alongside the same old railroad track I'd walked on toward California. As we sped down the highway, I kept a cavalier eye on it, allowing myself a gamut of emotions for the system that had failed to hold or save me. The one thing that made me feel better was that my mom had assured me Dad had given up drinking. I'd settle into my old life because I was stronger now. In the last two years, I'd been tossed into a mental institution with rapists, locked in a dark closet, and bathed in ice cold water. It felt as though I had been to a bloodless war and back. *I'm ready for this*, I chanted to myself as Marla drove down the long stretch of highway.

I was embarrassed that I was going back. I knew in those moments—and I still know—that I had failed. I sat in the passenger seat of the car, listening to the Beach Boys belt out "Kokomo," watching the line of trees alongside the road sway, the shiny edges of the track barb in and out.

When I took my last step out of the Social Services car, I was overcome with emotion, humbled. I was telling the truth, but everyone around me thought I was lying. Everyone, but my brother. He knew I was telling the truth.

I came home from war that day; nothing else mattered. The truth didn't matter to me anymore. The only hope I had of anyone loving me unconditionally was my parents. I surrendered to that hope. I imagined myself holding up my hands, waving a tiny white flag on a stick, whispering into the air, "I surrender." An idea crystalized in my mind; maybe we could be a happy family, maybe the fighting, bickering, and hostility was all behind us. But the idea snuffed itself out before I made it to the first step.

Bubba came out to greet us. "Hey, knucklehead," I said as I softly punched him.

He now towered over me and softly punched me back. "Glad you're home." He leaned over and hugged me.

Bubba and I both wanted a fresh start, so Mom was able to get us into the school I had been attending the next town over. It was a bigger school, so we both blended in seamlessly. Part of the agreement of my return was my father and I were to attend counseling together. I initially felt it might be good for him. He arranged for the counselor to come to our home. It turned out they knew each other, because Dad delivered his packages—which was why my father chose him. He had already informed his friend that I only ran away because I'd been afraid to accept my punishment for my failing grades in school.

During the "sessions" in our home, I had to patiently wait, while they talked about golf, fishing, hunting, boats, the weather, and, on occasion, packages. At the end of the last visit, the counselor asked me if I understood how serious it was that I had run away. Dad locked his eyes on me. It was the same gaze that for years made me feel like a deer in headlights and froze my insides too. I couldn't speak. I only nodded as the counselor said, "Good, good. Just make sure you try harder in school. You don't have to run away from home every time you make a bad grade."

In an act of celebration, upon my return home, my parents purchased new wardrobes for themselves and two coach tickets to Las Vegas. Bubba and I stayed home together, and Gabby, who was nine years old now, stayed with a neighbor. We would have loved to have gone to the Grand Canyon, to see what the Colorado River had carved for us, but Dad explained that there was only enough money for them to travel.

"We'll be sure to bring back plenty of pictures," Mom said. "Pictures are almost the same thing as going."

Bubba and I got along great when our parents weren't around. We watched movies, chatted over popcorn, and cooked our own meals. As it got closer to the time for our parents to return, so did the solemnness.

"Is it wrong to pray for a plane to crash?" Bubba asked me one evening.

I looked up at him. Was it wrong to wish for God to kill off a couple hundred people, just so we wouldn't have to see our parents anymore? I had to admit to myself that I secretly prayed for the same thing, although I hadn't put it in my sole. I knew it was wrong. Never had I wished for illness or death to befall someone. I felt justified, though, because I prayed for everyone but my parents to live and get settlements from a lawsuit, so they could buy nice houses and put their kids through college.

After a few seconds, I answered, "Yes, it is wrong. I can't believe you were thinking that."

———

EVEN THOUGH I HAD spent almost two years in foster care and Mom and Dad now made slight efforts to be better parents, life was pretty much the same. Dad came back from Las Vegas drinking booze again. Mom, who no longer worked outside the home, was still glued to books. Dad still came home grumpy, steering clear of me, because he was ticked off I had ratted him out. As horrible as life with my parents was, though, it was still better than foster care. Dad's eyes no longer glazed over when he looked at me. But there was something in the way that he'd brush by me, not acknowledging me, that made me realize I still didn't belong. The fantasy of being part of this family would never be my reality. Dad didn't yell at me for turning him in; he seemed to relish in the fact that it was all over, like an obstacle course he had won. Foster care was never mentioned again.

Dad seized on the opportunity of my running away from home. He made sure everyone knew that I indeed ran away because of bad grades. I was the spawn of the Devil, a fabricator. By the time his narrative made its way around town, everything that had happened to me was nothing more than hogwash.

I sat next to a girl in the cafeteria at my new school, who remembered me from my old school, where Mr. LeBlanc taught. We chatted for a few minutes, before she commented, "Aren't you the one who ran away from home?"

I nodded.

"My mom said you claimed your dad abused you, but she sells Tupperware, and he delivers our packages. She said he's not capable of doing the things you claimed."

"Because he delivers your packages?"

She picked up her tray and walked away, without even answering.

I studied my tray.

I didn't have the confidence to try to immobilize and crush Dad's narrative of events. He had already spread it from one end of the parish to the other. People gawked at me now, called me a liar. The memories of what he did to me still haunted me, and now to add insult to injury, I had to deal with people gossiping about it. It was hard to hold my head up. Dad had defined me to the town, to my mother, and to myself. But at the time I didn't realize just how much control he still had over me.

Everyone around him absorbed his words about me. My mother bore witness. I had become nothing more than a wicked interloper in their home, a stranger with whom they were burdened. I could no longer be trusted. My grades had testified to the world that they were speaking the truth. Dad made sure everyone around him knew there was a victim, but it wasn't me: it was *him*.

A few months into my senior year, I knew I was in trouble. Not only had I purposefully dumbed myself down in high school, but I had also missed a lot of school during my stint in foster care. My English teacher read one of my essays aloud during class and told everyone that in twenty years of teaching, it was the best paper she had ever read. It helped my self-esteem and my English grade, but I struggled in the other classes.

I wanted to join a club or organization, so I could feel that I was part of something but was told by all the worthwhile ones that I should have joined a few years earlier. I wasn't athletic, so I didn't try out for any sports. I wanted to attend the Air Force Academy after graduation but was told that because I had missed so much school and hadn't been a part of any groups, that it wasn't worth the time spent trying to gain admittance. *What if I can't get into college?* I made an appointment with an advisor and told her my predicament.

"You can't just waltz into the twelfth grade and expect everything to be handed to you on a silver platter," she said. "What have you been doing for the past four years?" As she waited for a response, her expression was cool, stoic. She sighed and crossed her arms, as though for the past few years I had coasted along, doing hardly anything, just waiting for a free ride. I could see she was aggravated. I wanted to tell her I had been busy surviving. Instead, I shrugged. She said my time was up; she had another appointment. I looked at the clock. We had another ten minutes. I gathered my books and left.

I didn't know what to do. I asked my mom for advice, but she said it wasn't her problem, that no one had helped her to make decisions either. "You know, Tracie," she said, "not everything is about you."

Ms. LeBlanc was my accounting teacher and tried to help me the best she could. She was everything Mr. LeBlanc had said she was and more. They each had their own comical characteristics, but it was obvious he was the storyteller, and she was the story. She had a natural whimsical nature and never seemed to stress about anything. She told me that she was sorry that foster care had not worked out for me and encouraged me to finish school and earn my diploma when I said that I wanted to give up. She also said that things have a way of working themselves out—just like Molly had once told me.

I WANTED TO KEEP making progress in my life, so I decided to take the next step, which was the one thing Bubba had already passed me up on: getting a driver's license. There was only one obstacle I had to overcome. I didn't know how to drive. True to his promise of buying me a car if I returned home, Dad bought me a small Isuzu I-Mark, on the condition that I pay for half of it. It had standard transmission, something I had never attempted before.

Dad taught me how to drive it. That's the way to learn how to drive a car, he told me, as he banged his foot on the clutch and switched the gear. He said, "Everything you drive after this will be a piece of cake."

A week before I was to take my driving test, Dad came home from work and tossed a manual into my lap. "What is this?" I asked looking up.

"It is the driver's handbook for the company I work for. Study it."

"But it's not on the test," I countered.

"It doesn't matter. Driving isn't a test," he barked, then his voice softened. "You are going to do over and above, just like I always taught you."

I flipped through the manual. Images of large, brown box trucks with bubble fronts jumped out at me. One page had bold letters that shouted not to go in reverse. Go forward. Always forward. I stopped on a page that was captioned: "Get the Big Picture." The illustration showed a driver zooming in with his eyes about a half a mile in front of him.

"I read this thing several times. Know what is in front of you, whether it is close or far away," Dad grinned enthusiastically. "Remember, always have an escape plan."

I cocked my head and listened for the next half hour as he settled into a lecture on driving, according to the standards set forth in the pages. This manual was the only thing needed to pass the driving test, that and the expert tutelage passing through my father's lips. As I studied the pools of blue in his eyes that were in deep contrast to the redness of his skin, I was struck by the irony in the moment: Dad handed me a manual that taught me how to successfully press forward, position myself to always be aware of what lurked ahead, stay focused on potential danger, and be prepared to get out of that situation. But the same person who handed me the manual to succeed was also the same person who had spent my entire life trying to make me crash and burn.

A few months after I got my driver's license, I decided it would be great to spend some time with Gabby. I had snatched a flyer the day before from a convenience store announcing a circus would be in town. It was a fall morning. Auburn leaves were scattered throughout the neighborhood.

"Do you want to go to the circus?" I asked.

She clapped her hands in excitement and wondered if she could invite Jake, the boy next door who was the same age as she was. I told her that if his mom gave him permission, that he could come. She did, so the three of us piled in my car. Once we arrived, I bought them both cotton candy and drinks, and we took our seats. Elephants paraded around in a circle under the big tent, heaving their giant bodies up to pose. Clowns walked on stilts and stuffed themselves into tiny cars. Different acts performed for over an hour. When the show ended, I told the kids we could go again the next time it was in town. We listened to the radio and sang ourselves into a happy stupor all the way home.

The next day, Mom told me that Jake's mom had punished him for going to the circus with me. But he had permission, I told her. "He did have permission to go to the circus," she said. "Just not with *you*. Jake's mom thought your father was bringing them. She didn't want him to be alone with you."

I shrugged and pretended not to care as I stumbled to my room. I couldn't believe that I had been judged so harshly by the neighbor. I closed my eyes and remembered how my dad had cracked drywall with my brother's body. How he had slammed my mother's body on the ground so hard it sounded like an explosion, snapping her leg. She was in a cast for months after that. I remembered all the times he had crept in my room at night, his hands roaming across my chest. *How many times had it been?* So many times, it made my head thrum just at the thought.

The fact was, I was upset by it, but laughed out loud when I realized how ironic the whole thing was. Jake had permission to go with my dad. Jake had permission to go with a *child molester*, but not the person who had spent eight years mustering up the courage to report him.

CHAPTER 20:

MOVING OUT

I walked past the television. The news was on. There was something familiar about the face floating on the screen. I tilted my head at it, trying to remember. The story that had lived dormant in a corner of my mind for over a year, surfaced, slowly at first, then began clubbing my brain with the memory. I remembered the night I had to go out with Amy and Greg. How she told me my life would be shattered because I told Kate about it. Two weeks later, I was gone. A person from that story was on the television. It was Greg. He had his own story now: he'd stabbed his mother, stabbed his brother, shot his father in the chest, then torched the house. He was seventeen.

His face was on all the news channels. And *boom*, just like that, the entire world knew about Greg. There had been something wrong with him after all. I'd known it. Felt it. The moment for truth was long gone. No one cared about the night in the parking lot anymore. I looked around to share what I knew about Greg. But the room was empty. Mom was in her room reading. I stood alone, feeling bad that Greg had murdered his family and ashamed that I hadn't been able to help him with whatever problem he'd had.

I scratched Greg a letter and told him I was bringing him personal care items. The next week, I bought him some things: toothpaste, a toothbrush, soap, shampoo, a couple reams of paper and a few pens. I put all of it, along with some cash, in a bag. I was going to help Greg, and I wanted answers. But mostly, he was a connection to a past I had pushed in the back of my mind. It pulsed inside my brain, brought back to life by gruesome murders.

I drove to the jail. I walked through metal detectors and steel doors. They clanged shut behind me. My breath caught in my chest. Memories clawed and fought inside my skull. It was the same clanging sound from when I had been locked up. I was led to a cubicle with a glass window. It had a beige phone sitting in a cradle. Greg appeared, shackled.

His hair was longer, unkempt, but he still had the same boyish grin. We both picked up a phone.

"I brought you some things," I said.

"Thank you," he replied. A few moments passed. He stared vacantly at the wall behind me. "My brother's body was preserved by the waterbed, you know. The stab marks were still there." His eyes watered. "I didn't get to tell him bye."

Greg had already confessed to stabbing his brother. I didn't know what to make of it, so I asked him if anyone else came to see him. He said only one aunt. Everyone else wanted him to die. I shifted uncomfortably on my stool.

"I brought you about a thousand sheets of paper," I said.

He raised an eyebrow. "Why?"

I wasn't sure if Greg understood he would be in jail for the rest of his life, but I didn't mention that he needed to make the thousand sheets last a lifetime.

"You need to write your story, Greg." Lights above reflected off the square glass. I leaned in closer with the phone, the pitch of my voice dropping low, almost to a whisper. "Everyone needs their story heard."

I knew it was true. I'd dragged around paper my entire life. I had it in my shoes, begged for notebooks and loose leaf and binders for Christmas and birthdays, my fingers always scribbling moments down. He seemed to come from a better family than I had. He had a family that loved him, and he murdered them. I don't know why, suddenly, I felt compassion for him. He and Amy had ruined my life. Why, after seventeen years of abuse, was I trying to help someone worse than my dad? Greg was, beyond any doubt, a murderer. Maybe it was because so many people had judged me harshly. It made me not want to judge anyone, not even a killer. I put the receiver back on the cradle and nodded bye.

I never spoke to Greg again.

A few days later, I found Bubba stuffing his clothing into bags. He and Dad had been quarreling, back and forth, for the last few days, and Bubba had had enough. I didn't say anything at first but paced my way through my parents' mobile home. Finally, I went to stand in his doorway. His guitar case that he sometimes hid chewing tobacco in was still in its regular place leaning up against a wall, as were most things that had value.

"I don't want to take anything that's going to remind me of this place," he said when he saw me glancing around his room. He continued packing.

I went into the living room to see what my mom had to say. She was folded on a recliner, reading a *Little House on the Prairie* book, and seemed to be oblivious to what was happening.

"Did you know that Bubba is moving out?" I asked.

"Well, I can't stop him," she said as she turned a page and continued reading.

"You aren't going to do anything?"

"Yes, I am. I'm going to finish my book in another room." She jerked to her feet and pushed past me.

Bubba was still waiting for his ride when Dad came home. I was waiting for a giant explosion from Dad, but the blowup was small. He was only concerned with getting Bubba legally emancipated so he wouldn't get stuck with paying the state child support again. They agreed to meet somewhere the next day and get the paperwork done.

When his ride pulled up and honked the horn, Bubba looked at me as if to say, *"This is it."* I reached out to him and hugged him close, but not long. Dad was in the background, red-faced, with a vein pounding on the side of his neck, telling Bubba that it was time to get the hell out. I knew Bubba was leaving for the same reasons that I had. I didn't blame him, but I didn't want him to go.

After he left, I took a long shower and cried so the tears would run down the drain with the rest of the water. I had so many emotions about his departure, but I didn't want my parents to see how much it upset me. Bubba meant more to me than I ever realized, and now he had left for good.

Something had pushed me to walk, pray, and believe, but a totally different something had pushed Bubba. I don't know for sure what pushed me to the edge, to leave at the age of fifteen, any more than Bubba knew what it was that pushed him out that same door at sixteen. Now I was seventeen, eleven months older than Bubba. I was starting to understand that we would always be tethered by trauma, both of us trying to escape from it. The only difference was that I had walked into the light full of hope and promise. Bubba, with no plan at all and not a clue where he was going, stared deep into the dark void, and pitched himself in.

I WASN'T QUITE SURE what I wanted to do with my life, but Dad was pressuring me to start earning an income. I had recently graduated high school. My grades weren't good enough for scholarships. I applied at a Fruit of the Loom plant that had opened just down the road from our house and got the job. When the manager told me that I would be making twelve dollars an hour, once I reached full production, I nearly fell out my chair.

After I told Dad, he dragged out a calculator and wire notebook. He started calculating my monthly rent for living with them, as well as car insurance. I still would come out with enough every check to build a little savings. I had been terrified of the adult world my whole life and had never imagined that one day I could get a job, straight out of high school, making serious money.

Not only was the money great, but I also loved working there. My job was sewing sleeves onto T-shirts, and I cranked out approximately 1,200 of them a day. Hundreds of machines were lined up in neat little rows, each row doing something different. Bundles of flat material with tickets attached started out at the front of the line. After each person did their part, they would write their assigned number on the top of the ticket, tear off a numbered stub from the bottom portion, and glue it to a production sheet. Then, the bundle would get tossed forward to the next person, until, by the time it came to me—I was called a "set sleeve"—it would become a full shirt with sleeves and hems. I tossed each shirt into a little shirt trough as I finished it.

When all sixty shirts in that bundle were complete, I would tie up the bundle with a neat little bow on top and carry it to an inspector. If a shirt wasn't up to company standards, it got sent back for repairs. There were also inspectors walking throughout the building, randomly checking ten or more shirts at a time from each employee. On average, each bundle got checked at least a half-dozen times from start to finish. Quality was essential, but so was production. The slowest employees got paid less, and if your quality wasn't up to par, you got a write-up. Pretty soon, I was at peak production making twelve dollars an hour. From each paycheck I paid rent to my parents, insurance, food, and gas. I always had enough to save and usually enough to buy a pair of Guess jeans or a new pair of shoes too. For the first time in my life, I felt like I was on my way.

AFTER ABOUT A YEAR at Fruit of the Loom—working forty-eight hours a week—dark bracelets of wrinkles started to form around my wrists because of the unforgiving labor. I wore a face mask as often as I could stand to, but lint would gather on my clothes and my hair. As I breathed, it would settle in my lungs and even up my nose. On the other hand, working in a hot factory with hundreds of women had sharpened my appreciation for women of all backgrounds and ages. We were all one and worked as a team to get the job done quickly and efficiently. This was my favorite part of the job. Being part of something unified to accomplish a goal. I had spent so much of my life isolated and alone, that I just enjoyed the presence of other women. During this time, I honed my skills of working quickly and accurately. It was easy to tell who was having a bad day and who was having a great day, so I learned to adjust my attention accordingly.

There were days where I chatted all day to anyone who would listen. On those days, I sewed fewer shirts, made less money, and my supervisor joked around that if I'd shut my yapper, I'd get more work done. Then there were days when I'd walk in with my serious face on—I knew I had a bill due—and I'd put a mask on that covered my mouth, so I wouldn't talk and could be productive. Occasionally, I would pull the mask to the side, scarf down a mouthful of fresh air and continue setting sleeves, without missing a beat. My supervisor figured out my strategy and when he would see me wearing a mask, he'd walk by and whisper in my ear what a great job I was doing, maybe clap my shoulder if he was feeling extra generous. I'd just nod without even looking up, lest he cost me ten cents or more with the distraction.

The thrumming of the machines around me, the constant sliding of metal chairs from people moving their bundles to the next table, the blowing of lint-covered machines with the air hoses, and the occasional burst of laughter from a group of people chatting it up as they worked, became my new perception of how the real world ticked around the clock. I liked it.

MOM STARTED WORKING AT Fruit of the Loom too. Dad suggested we ride to work together. This made me uncomfortable. Sometimes, she would have a shiner or a split lip, and I didn't want to be seen with her. Once she would slip the car into a parking space, I would slide down in the seat or put a book in front of my face and walk ten steps behind her as we entered the building. Sometimes, I would say that I left something in the car. Even on the days that she didn't have dark circles around her eyes, I knew there would be days where she would, and I didn't want anyone associating me with the woman who had lilac-colored raccoon eyes. I was afraid people would figure out my past that I locked up so tightly. I never mentioned to anyone I worked with that I had ever been abused or in foster care. Being normal was important to me, and I didn't want her to blow my cover.

I had a modest savings account, but it wasn't growing fast enough. Between taxes, health insurance, and other deductions, my checks weren't quite as big as I liked them to be. Now that I had a car—Dad paid for half—I had the freedom to come and go as I chose, so I found a church to go to and spent as much time there as I could. Often, I went to movies alone, or would go walk around department stores or the mall to pass time, until I absolutely had to go home.

One day, Mom announced that Dad wasn't getting along with some of the people he worked with, so he was transferring over an hour away. They would move within a month.

"But what about me?" I asked. "Where am I going to live?" After all my expenses, I wasn't sure if I could afford to live on my own. I was barely saving money as it was.

"I'm sure you'll find something," she replied. "We have to think of us. You'll be fine."

I went to visit my cousin Josephine and expressed my concern to her. I was terrified of being homeless. "Hey, don't worry about it." She stroked my hair, then placed my hand in hers. "I'll see what I can do." A few days later, she called to tell me that her mother-in-law said that I could rent a room from her at a reasonable rate until I found a place I could afford. It was a great relief. I slipped another paper in my shoe.

I want to be financially independent.

The room was in an old plantation home that had been featured in a book about haunted houses. The home was slathered with history, dating back to before the Civil War. It had a tunnel—someone had long ago sealed it off—that could be accessed from a secret entrance in the closet. If you opened the closet and ran your fingers along the edge of the drywall, eventually you grabbed a small hidden lever that opened a secret door. About ten feet into the tunnel was a wall of concrete, so you could go no farther. Ann, Josephine's mother-in-law, told me that I could stay upstairs by myself, in the haunted part. On more than one occasion, I walked downstairs, only to have Josephine jump out and scare me. Just like Jack used to, I found myself chasing her with whatever I could get my hands on.

Ann spent a great deal of time creating and painting ceramic busts and talking on the phone. We'd spend most evenings together. Josephine and her husband were living across the street with her three young boys. Ms. LeBlanc and Molly were right; life did have a way of working itself out. Slowly, I started to blend in with Josephine's family.

I only saw my parents sporadically, usually on holidays, when I had to drive an hour to see them. Mostly, I wanted to see Gabby. They never once came to see me. Dad called only a few times, and this did not get past Ann.

One day, she motioned for me to come sit next to her. She said my parents were toxic to me and that I had some tough decisions to make. She sat across from me as she said this and glared at me, unblinking, as though everyone in the world but me knew this.

I stared at her blankly. I didn't understand.

"Tracie," she said in her signature raspy voice, "you know that I'm not one to get into anyone's business. But I've noticed that your mother has never contacted you or come to see you. Not even once."

"Yes?"

"You need to know that that is not a normal relationship between a mother and a daughter. Right? I call my daughters no less than twice a week and never go more than two or three weeks without seeing them. It's worth the drive to see your daughter."

I sat quietly, wordlessly shifting on my seat.

Ann said that she could tell my parents didn't care about me on the same level that I wanted them to care. She told me this as she squeezed my shoulder, and she did it so lovingly I wanted to rest my face on her hand.

To make me understand, she picked up the phone right then and dialed her daughter who lived about fifty miles away. They spoke for several minutes. She hung up the phone, looked at me, and said, "It's that simple."

I tried to wrap my mind around that. *If it's so simple, how come my mother has never done it?*

―

AFTER ABOUT A YEAR of living with Ann and her husband, I moved out on my own for the first time. Ann called me regularly and even came by a few times to visit me at my apartment. I really appreciated her. My own mother never once visited me or called. I made attempts to call her, hoping she would catch on and try to form a relationship, but she never did. Ann died of cancer a few years later, and I missed her terribly. Everyone who showed that they cared for me seemed to disappear.

Being on my own with no family was lonely, and I found myself not wanting to be cooped up in my apartment. I had spent so much time in the last few years under the control of other people that I wanted to be outdoors when I wasn't at work. I felt like I didn't even want the earth holding me down. I took flying lessons on Saturdays, joined a gym, and took a handful of taekwondo classes.

There was a dim hollowness in me, a desire for a family. I saw my parents on major holidays. On that first Thanksgiving on my own, I didn't realize that most restaurants would be closed. I ended up eating a day-old sausage biscuit from a gas station and then went home to watch parades on television. It was then that I realized that I needed to figure out how to continue moving forward in my life if I didn't want to be alone forever.

One day, Josephine asked me if I would watch her boys while she ran some errands. I still lived in an apartment and didn't have much to entertain them, so I bought some cheap cans of shaving cream for them to play with. They had a blast playing outside, making shaving cream castles, and shaving cream roads for their trucks. I sat on a lawn chair and read a book. When they were finished, they asked for a picture of their shaving cream city. As I was backing up, staring into the camera's viewfinder, I bumped into a man with deep blue eyes and golden blond hair, neatly parted to the side. Muscular and toned from the sun, he was handsome and rugged, with broad shoulders that gave him the appearance of an athlete.

"I'm sorry," I stammered.

He grinned a gorgeous smile and said, "No problem."

We both looked at each other awkwardly for a moment before he asked if they were my children.

"Oh, no, not mine. I just borrow and return."

"You seem to be a creative babysitter." He laughed as he pointed at the shaving cream city in front of my apartment.

"It's cheap entertainment, but I think I have to clean it up before I land in trouble. I seem to have a knack for that."

"You don't look like the type of girl who would get into any trouble," he commented. "But I have to admit, you are the only person here with a stoop covered in shaving cream."

"I'm surprised one of the neighbors hasn't called security. Plus, their mom isn't going to be happy trying to get all that shaving cream out of their hair." I chuckled, thinking about what great payback this was for all the times Josephine had frightened me. "Yep," I said with satisfaction, "it'll keep her busy for a while."

He told me his name was Mark. We talked for a few minutes, before he went on his way. One evening, about a week later, we ran into each other at the mailboxes. Our boxes were near each other. He backed away so I could pass by. I cautiously approached with my key, as though the earth would open up and swallow us both if I approached too close. After I retrieved my mail, he asked me if I remembered him. I nodded. Then he asked me if the kids got all the shaving cream off.

"I think it took a few baths. It will probably be a while before their mom asks me to babysit again."

We stood at the mailbox and talked until dusk, the amber rays from the evening slowing fading away. I said that I needed to get back home. After a moment of silent awkwardness, he asked me if he could come over sometime, and I agreed. It then occurred to me that this might be an actual date, and when I came to this realization, I dropped my mail all over the ground.

He appeared at my doorway a few days later and said he wanted to sit and talk. I bought ice cream earlier, so I scooped some into bowls. We settled onto the sofa, and he asked me about my life while we ate. I had not shared my foster care experience with anyone before. I'd always felt ashamed of my life, the past. Foster care had been my biggest failure. I had not succeeded in being loved, so for years, kept it hidden, like a misspelled tattoo. I confided him my secret past, sketching a picture of what I had been through. Mark listened intently.

When I finished, there was a long pause; the only sounds were our spoons scraping sharply against the ceramic bowls. I braced myself for what he might say. Mark was kinder and gentler to me than anyone had been in a long time; if he was overwhelmed by my past, he didn't let on. I felt I could finally trust someone. The waters rose just enough for me to dip my toe in.

"You have an incredible story," he said after a few moments. He held his hand up for me to take it. I lifted mine slowly, nervously, as if I were reaching for a flame. I'd never held another man's hand before. I almost jerked it away, afraid of being burned, but my loneliness was more than I could bear. My hand sank into his.

I grinned. The water felt fine.

Before long, Mark and I were spending all our evenings and weekends together. He bought me a bicycle, and we biked all over town. Some days we would load up his boat with fishing rods and tackle and bump down the road to the nearest waterway. I didn't particularly like to fish, but I loved being with Mark. We haunted waterholes where the fishing was good, bike trails that weren't too bumpy, and small hole-in-the-wall restaurants that I had never heard of. Late evenings, we took long walks, our fingers intertwined, talking about our lives underneath a velvety black sky, before parting ways for the night.

Mark owned an old souped-up Chevy pickup with a glossy fire engine-red finish. Every weekend, he tinkered under the hood trying to make it go faster and run smoother—or sometimes just run. I'd often wander over to his apartment and sit on the curb, hugging my knees, while he talked about the engine, the carburetor, or the belt that kept slipping.

Mark took me dancing on a Friday night and held my hand as I stepped all over his shoes. When I showed him the dreams I had hidden in my soles, he wrote his name on a sliver of paper and pressed it in my shoe. He told me that my flaws, my little quirks, made him love me more and more every day. Being loved by someone, unconditionally, made my life feel like it had been calibrated, as though my entire life, up until that point, had been out of balance.

I imagined myself introducing Mark to my parents. But when I thought of him meeting my dad, that image fizzled out. Even at the age of twenty-three, I was still trying to figure out things about my family. I pictured my dad tensely sizing up Mark as he shook his hand. Smiling, charismatic. The second Mark and I would leave, things would change. As powerful as an eagle's talon, Dad's paranoia would swoop in and latch on to his brain, point out the risk of another man hanging around. A darkness would build up in his eyes as he'd spend the evening transforming. He would get hooked on black thoughts and suspicions of Mark.

After a lifetime of knowing my father, I knew this is how he would react. It would have been nice to entertain a reality where I introduced Mark to my parents, and they would be genuinely excited for me. But in my reality, I had to warn my boyfriend not to hug my mother, for any reason. Although chances were, after their introduction, Mom got beaten anyway; after Dad spent the evening imagining that Mark, the love of my life—a country boy whose passion was old pickup trucks and fishing—was somehow a threat.

Chapter 21:

The Fractured Daughter

———

One cloudless Saturday, Mark announced that he was taking me fishing in his boat at a nature preserve called Lake Martin. Lake Martin was a swampland full of egrets, herons, bullfrogs, turtles, alligators, and cypress trees with hanging Spanish moss. It seemed like a nice place to go.

As we drove down the gravelly road, toward the boat ramp, giant alligators—some over six-feet long—lay stretched out in the shallow marshy edges. We stopped to take a few pictures of them. On the water, Mark patiently baited my hooks and untangled my line from trees, stumps, and clumps of hydrilla. He reeled in my fish. When I tried to cast my line out and hooked him in the neck, he started tossing my line out as well.

Late that evening, we witnessed an alligator lunge at a heron that was swaggering along the edge of a small island. "It's the circle of life," Mark told me. He also informed me that there were over five-hundred alligators in the lake. When dusk came, he said it was time to head back.

After he got the boat close enough to the bank, he helped me out and put a rope in my hand. "Hold this," he said. I didn't see the need to stand there, holding the rope, since there were no waves to carry the boat away, so I laid it down neatly on the mushy ground, and walked quietly behind Mark.

When he got in the truck, I hopped in on the other side. "What are you doing? I told you to hold the rope," he said.

"I did hold it, and then I put it on the ground. It's humid out there."

He put the truck in reverse and floored it to the ramp. "Hey, you're going awfully fast," I said, while looking out the rear window. "Also, I think someone stole your boat. It's gone."

"No, it floated away. That was the purpose of holding the rope," he said as he jumped out the truck. The boat was floating peacefully near some cypress trees as Mark sprinted onto a side dock, ripped his shoes and socks off, and dived in.

"Mark," I shouted, "there are alligators in there!"

The boat was about a hundred feet out. I cringed as numberless pairs of eyes floated up to the water's surface to stare at him. I couldn't bear to watch him become part of the circle of life. Mark was going to get eaten by an alligator, and it would be my fault. When he made it to the boat, without becoming alligator food, I was elated.

He cranked the motor and headed back in. When he stepped out of the boat and onto the dock, he was dripping and covered in moss. I reached out for the rope.

He shook his head. "No, I don't want you to hold the rope anymore. But I do have something for you."

He squeezed his hands into the pocket of the cut-off jean shorts he was wearing and pulled out a square box. He knelt, rope still in hand, and opened it. Inside was a ring.

"You were right. You told me you were trouble, and you are. But that's what I love about you. I've been carrying this around for a while, waiting for the right moment. I guess this is it. I hope you say yes."

He took the little ring out of the dripping box and placed it onto my finger. I nodded and then quietly whispered, "Yes." What else could I say to the man who had just braved the company of a five-hundred alligators because of me?

Mark and I seemed to be made for each other. We often took long drives in his old Chevy. Sometimes I would yell, "Stop the truck!" and run out to pick up a turtle trying to cross the road and place it out of harm's way or save a stray kitten or dog and bring it home, until we could find a place for it. He loved standing over the stove to make gumbo or smothered chicken over rice, and I loved eating it. When I told him more about my foster care history, I confessed that I felt like a failure, first with my biological family and then with my foster families. He told me that I wasn't a failure but had beautiful flaws and was strong. He said that over and over: I was strong.

———

WE GOT MARRIED ABOUT a year after we met, and eventually, I realized just how much the love of my life disregarded his own safety. Time after time, I yelled at Mark to be careful, moments before he tore, dislocated, or stabbed some part of his body. One day, he badly cut his hand while working in his shop, and instead of going to the emergency room to get stitches, he searched through the greasy oil rags that were lying around. After he found the greasiest one—so as not to ruin any of his good grease rags—he used some electrical tape to secure the rag over the gash.

He fell off a building and shattered his face and back. Fell off another building and crushed his leg. Seven surgeries. Flipped a four-wheeler and broke his clavicle. Tore his rotator cuff four times. Picked a scab on his knee (from a knee surgery) and developed colitis. A green line was inching up his leg, and finally, I demanded he go to the hospital. The doctor said I brought Mark "in the nick of time," or he might not have made it to the next day. When I was about to receive an epidural during excruciating contractions before the birth of our son, I looked over to see the needle had been dropped on a silver tray; the nurses were fanning smelling salts under Mark's nose. He had passed out when he saw the size of the needle.

I bought first-aid kits and dropped them discreetly throughout the home—under the sofa, in a kitchen drawer, behind the cat. Each time he got hurt, I remembered how he once jumped into a lake full of alligators to rescue a boat. I soon realized that Mark's flaw was being reckless with himself, and we would have to be strong together.

My son, Dillon, was born a year after we were married. He became my joy and made me forget every bad thing I had been through in my life. I found my headaches that had quietly thrummed in my head, since I was a teenager, seemed to vanish as though a magician had waved a magic wand over my head. Dillon was bubbly and happy, and I felt like I had finally hit life's jackpot.

Mark and I lived off just one salary and invested the other. We saved enough cash to buy a mobile home and three acres of land. By this time, I realized that I didn't want to work in a sewing factory anymore. I had ambitions, dreams. I wanted to be my own boss. Before long, with our saved money, we were flipping houses. After a year of living on the acreage, we sold the land for more than double what we paid for it and moved into a small mobile home park. Within two years, we owned the park. Eventually, we owned all the mobile homes in the park and rented them out. I quit my job at the factory.

We bought a large foreclosed home and, because of my time in foster care, Mark and I both felt we needed to give back. Our first three foster children were brothers; a four-year-old and two-year-old twins. One climbed the banister going up the staircase every time I turned my back. We sprayed each other with water guns and the garden hose, which may or may not have been in the house. When one of the kids objected to getting the inside of the house wet, I sprayed him as well. "We can dry the cabinets," I told him. "This is forever." At times, eggs were involved. We cleaned it all up as a family.

When my son was eight years old, he told me that he wanted to live near his grandparents and cousins. I'd been longing for a closer relationship with my mother, so I mulled the idea over. I discussed it with Mark. We decided to sell our home and rental business to move closer to my family. Excitedly, I called my parents and told them our plan. Neither responded and changed the subject.

Months later, by phone, I confronted each of them, separately, about why they didn't want me to move closer to them. Mom blamed Dad. "You know how he is," she told me, before changing the subject. I hung up with her and called him the next day while she was at work.

"It would be different if you were Gabby," Dad said, "and wanted to live next door to us. Your mom is so obsessed with her, she would demand we sell everything and buy enough land for us and Gabby to build on." The air was sucked out of my lungs so quickly, that I had to sit down to listen to more. He must have taken a long drag on a cigarette because it was a few moments before he spoke again. "The problem," he continued, "is you aren't Gabby."

The instant the words slipped from his lips, I knew I'd remember them forever—not just the words but the cruel moment. I remember the creak of a door. Footsteps. I remember my son tugging my shirt, asking for a snack, his cool hands working their way up to my face, asking why I was crying. I remember crying. I don't remember telling Dad bye, but I must have.

After I hung up with him, I folded myself on the sofa and bawled for hours. It didn't matter how much I loved my mother, how I'd spent countless nights of my childhood whispering in the dark for her; no matter how much I called her on the phone just to hear her voice, I would always be the other daughter, the fractured one.

A few days later, I was shopping. There was a woman with black hair, back toward me, scanning a shelf for an item. From behind, she looked like Mom. I imagined it was her, so I crept closer, pretending to look on the same shelf. My heart pounded; adrenaline gushed through my body. Growing up, shopping with Mom hadn't been an option. She always had to be guarded from men. But those weren't special memories. It had felt like a job. As an adult, I wanted to be near her, shop with her, scan a shelf together, create memories.

The woman turned toward me and nodded, before pushing her cart further down. My eyes watered as she walked away. I remembered she wasn't my mother. Every time I phoned Mom and she mentioned that she went antiquing with Gabby, shopping with her, or had lunch together, Dad's words would echo loudly in my ear, like a drum perpetually beating in a loop. Long after we had given up on the idea of moving near my parents, long after my hair turned gray and I was still hovering near strange women looking at items on shelves, those words would pound out a continuous rhythm in my head: *You aren't Gabby.*

―

WHEN GRANDMA AVIS PASSED at the age of sixty-seven, my first thought was that she had died thinking I was a liar. She bought into the tales Dad wove about me, when he cried to anyone who would listen, that I had tried to destroy him over bad grades. I imagined she and Aunt Carol shook their heads about what a diabolical little thing I was. I had never tried to prove to her that I was a victim; after all, I had no proof. So, to the end, she believed my dad was the victim.

It was my own fault. Like everyone else in my family, I had allowed Dad to control the conversation about me. I had given him free reign to destroy my reputation. Not one person, including my mother, had ever asked my side of Dad's stories. Perhaps they didn't really want to know, or perhaps his blunted version of events was more interesting or simply easier to go along with. He had merely corrected his teenager, and the wicked little thing spread lies about him in retaliation.

My cousin Jack told me an interesting story a few months after Grandma died. He said the Christmas they rode with us to West Monroe in the back of the truck, something odd had happened. When Dad had taken him and Bubba for a ride in the truck, it was to scope out yards, so they could steal a three-wheeler. "I'm not sure if Bubba understood what was going on," Jack continued, "*but I did.*" He went on to say that a woman was parked on the side of the road, passed out, drunk. He said Dad got out the truck and lurched to the car. My father looked around to see if anyone was watching, then opened the door and groped the woman's chest. I gasped. Jack continued. Moments later, cops came from around a corner and asked Dad what he was doing. He responded that he was only trying to help her. The cops didn't believe him and hollered at him to leave. Jack said they went back to Grandma's after that. Then he paused and told me there was no doubt in his mind that Dad was going to sexually assault that woman. The cops showed up in the nick of time. Although I was shocked, I shouldn't have been. After all, he had done the same thing to me.

Several years later, Dad's mom passed away. I hadn't known her well but decided to go to the funeral. It was strange to sit on the pew, while her other grandchildren stood at the podium and talked about what a wonderful grandmother she had been. Bubba and I glanced at each other. We had barely known her name. The ceremony was held at the funeral home owned by my dad's aunt Patsy and uncle Tom—the same aunt and uncle who owned a monstrous house with an inground pool and slot machines that Dad never allowed us to visit. Aunt Patsy still had the same gentle voice and loving arms that embraced me when I was five years old. I wondered why Dad had kept us away from this beautiful woman who had, at one time, meant so much to me. The room was full of cousins who no longer remembered me. Time had taken its toll. I couldn't get Aunt Patsy off my mind. A month later, I called Mom. I told her I had enjoyed seeing Aunt Patsy again and would like to continue seeing her. I was going to go back for a visit. Without missing a beat, Mom said, "You can't. She died."

Shocked, I said, "What? When did this happen?"

"A few weeks ago."

I hung up and called the floral shop my aunt Patsy owned and worked at. A man answered the phone. I asked for Aunt Patsy. The man told me she was out to lunch. I asked if he was sure. He told me he had worked with her all morning on a floral arrangement.

I thanked him and hung up the receiver. I realized that my father was still spreading lies about me. My mother, the woman who had birthed me in her teens, stood at his side, supporting his account of events from the past. I was no longer their daughter but a holiday visitor. For some reason, they didn't want me having contact with Dad's family. I had started catching them in too many lies. It felt awkward.

Bubba and I also distanced from one another over the years. I found him to be harsh on his children but learned that it went on according to the say-so of my mother and father. I eventually tired of hearing whisperings about him. But instead of trying to get him help, I snapped at him.

After everything we had been through as children, I told him, he needed to do better. I went too far, and he breathed in the words I said, before I could snatch them back.

Bubba and I couldn't continue walking the same path, so we parted at the fork in the road of our lives. I was angry with him, but it was I who challenged him. I couldn't fix it, so I left it broken. We never spoke again.

Gabby married a man named Peter and had a son. Not long after Bubba and I stopped talking, she started pulling away from me as well. It became very difficult to hold conversations—she would avoid eye contact whenever I tried to talk to her and gave me only generic answers. It took me a while, but I believe I figured out what the problem was.

Mark and I didn't go often, but whenever we were at my parents' house, Dad would drone about what a horrible person Peter was, how he'd ripped them off on some remodeling work he'd done in their home, pointing out mistakes in the paint job. Mom would help him identify streaks and runs on the walls. After several visits of this, Mark—tired of hearing about it—offered to repaint their home for free. Dad was euphoric. Mark drove the hour-long round trip, every day for a week, until the job was complete.

I noticed, not long after that, Peter stopped talking to us. Then Gabby spoke to me as little as possible. One day I went to my parents' house, and she was there, playing a game on the computer. I tried to engage conversation with her, but she wouldn't look me in the eye and stayed focused on the screen, barely acknowledging me. I stood up to go play with her son, Tim, who was playing with a small ball instead of eating his lunch. I took it from him, as a game, and told him sassily it was mine. He screamed. I told him he could come home with me, and he'd have angel wings after a week. It was something my sister-in-law, Cathy, had often joked about with my own son. My response to Cathy was always fun, playful. "That's sounds perfect," I'd say. "Take him for *two* weeks."

I expected such a response from my sister, hoping it would lighten the mood. But Gabby gave me no such response. She jerked up from the computer and hollered at me to give Tim back the ball. It was the only full sentence she had spoken to me in months. She then went on to scream about how my son wasn't perfect either. I listened to my sister's rant. It seemed to be well-thought-out, so I figured, surely, it must be some sort of prank, and I waited for the punchline that never came. There was so much anger coming from her, it was shocking. *Where is all this anger coming from?*

My gaze shifted toward Dad, who had cast his eyes down at the floor, and for the first time in his life, had nothing to say. I felt as though he was the source and wondered if he had told Gabby and Peter that it was Mark's own idea to redo the paint job. Mark had only been trying to keep the peace. As her words rushed at me, I felt a strange sensation, of loss. This was the last time I would see my sister. I stood wordless, not replying, burying her in my mind. It was the day I lost her forever, this person I had loved from the moment she was born, this person I had done my best to protect. I began to sob, suffocating sobs, so hard that I couldn't speak; I snatched my keys and fled, bawling the entire way home.

The bond with my sister, already hovering on extinction from desuetude, ebbed itself out that evening, like the last flicker of a burnt-down candle. It broke my heart that she was gone from my life, but her life went on the same. A few months later, she announced to my parents that she was having a second child, and they were beyond themselves with elation. The baby was a girl.

Our estrangement was not without reason. My sister was born to a different set of parents; she has different memories than me. Because of the age gap, I had most of the memories. My memories started to be consistent around the age of eight, which was when Gabby was born. Mine are cradling her, singing to her, dancing with her little fingers wrapped around mine. Pushing her on her first bicycle, playing patty-cake over and over, until our palms were red. When she was a toddler, and Dad was beating Mom in another room, I would put cotton balls in her ears and make her giggle by running my finger along her spine, so she couldn't hear the screams. I remember the contrasting giggles as Mom howled in the background. Gabby's memories are of me fleeing home, coming back, leaving again. I was a stranger my dad called nuts and my mom shrugged off. Maybe I don't blame her for not knowing me, for not wanting to know me. Maybe I don't.

By the time she had reached an age where she could start cataloguing her own, I ran away from home. She had been seven years old. It was that same age Dad had started sexually abusing me. When I left, Dad became terrified of losing Gabby. He stopped drinking, tamped down his anger, didn't dare touch her. I'd questioned Gabby several times, probing her for answers, asking if anyone had ever touched her, or made her uncomfortable. She always said no, and to this day, I believe her. There is no doubt in my mind if I had not run away, Gabby would have been his next victim. That is the only reason I can think of that makes the whole foster-care experience worth it to me. No one in my family seems to remember my stint in foster care, but I'm sure the memory is in a remote corner of Dad's mind. It had been a close call for him.

At the age of eleven, I stood up for my mom by engaging my dad in a confrontation about his infidelity. In response, he placed a gun between us, its barrel ambiguously aimed at my baby sister. My mother continuously turned a cold shoulder to me, as though I never mattered. She sided with him for the things that happened to me. Even as I grew older, I didn't gain the confidence to quell the chronicle of lies my dad had constructed. I knew that he also had stories about my two siblings that I would raise an eyebrow of skepticism at, but because I had once pushed back, I would suffer the most.

Years passed, and my mother never once asked me what I had been through, before or during foster care. She never called me, nor showed an interest in my life—nor my son's, really. The great divide that had formed between my mother and me was so vast, so wide and deep, it seemed to go on forever, impassable. Who was I to want to be loved by her? No one. Eventually, she became a speck on the other side of a widening chasm. We were at an impasse. I was no longer willing to risk my mental well-being to attempt the struggle to get to her.

I realized why I hadn't followed my family to Baton Rouge after high school, why I had chosen to stay behind and make a life of my own. When my parents moved away, they'd taken the drama and chaos with them. Dad still beat Mom and held her accountable for every minute. He had long-retired with a back injury, going to her job once or twice a day, on the pretense of purchasing something—a tube of toothpaste in the morning, a bottle of shampoo after lunch.

Memories of foster care had faded, drowned by distance and time, but occasionally, one would rear up out the water. Dad, knowing those memories were tethered to me, would push me back down, taking foster care to the depths with me. He still belittled me to everyone in the family, told them I was nuts. A new generation was born, grandchildren. He told them I was the crazy daughter, the crazy sister, the crazy aunt. But what none of them knew was one day, long ago, I'd stood up to a Goliath in my life, their grandfather.

A raspy voice from the past echoed in my ear, gently reminding me that my family was toxic, that good mothers made time for their daughters. I closed my eyes and inhaled. I could almost smell the smoke from Ann's cigarette, the moment felt so real.

The last time I saw my parents, it was spring, Barack Obama was a newly elected president, and my siblings no longer talked to me.

I POURED MY ENERGY into real estate. Every house Mark and I flipped started out as a blank canvas for me. It was as if Dad, who pushed me to memorize words and passages and write long essays, had merely sent me on a wild goose chase. Learning had helped me, but the trauma associated with it had pushed me in a different direction.

The homes became symbolic of the life I once had: fist holes, broken furniture, dark rooms. The reality they sketched, of rage, poverty, loneliness—a forgotten world—breathed a sensation that emboldened the strong woman inside me. At one home, it had trash bags and tinfoil taped on the windows. I ripped them off with such intensity, Mark asked if I was okay.

When we were done remodeling the home, it was bright, the walls chalky white. I stood in the center and slipped on a pair of sunglasses. I once imagined I would be free from the darkness Dad had forced on us. I could now tint the world around me, but it would be on my terms.

There was something about broken homes with their fist holes and covered windows, their smoke-stained walls and shattered glass, tainted by someone's past, rich with potential, that made me realize I had taken the shattered pieces of my own past and made something beautiful out of it.

I considered myself an entrepreneur. My husband called me the brains behind the operation, and I called him the brawn. I'd find and negotiate the deals and design the inside, and he'd swoop in and gut the home, usually, and install new flooring, cabinets, fixtures, and paint.

At the end of each job, it was very satisfying to stand back and see what we had accomplished. As my footsteps echoed in the halls of the homes we remodeled, I was struck by memories of all the times Dad called me a failure, how he told Bubba and me that we would never amount to anything. He once told me I didn't want to succeed. Of course, I wanted to succeed. I had spent most of my life scrambling after pipe dreams, waiting for small beacons of light to burst from the darkness.

After Mark and I closed on our twentieth flip, I held the million-dollar check up to the light, stared at all the zeros, and one thought passed through my mind: *Who's amounted to something now? Me.*

Chapter 22:

Me Too

I was almost to my SUV when someone shouted my name. I turned to see who it was.

"I can't believe it's you! It's you!" shouted a homeless woman as she rushed to me.

At first, I panicked and almost ran because a strange person knew my name. But she grabbed both of my shoulders and beamed into my face.

"Greenie!" her voice boomed so loudly it seemed to reverberate across the whole city. My jaw fell open as my past came to me like rushing waters, nearly knocking the breath out my lungs.

"Lindsey?" I gasped, but then after a few seconds of searching her face for something to recognize, I realized she had the same old ear piercings in her ear, though her hair was natural gray now, not dyed black. I understood it really was her and screamed, *"Lindsey!"*

She let go of my shoulders and looked at my SUV and then back at me. "Well, it looks like you adapted to the world pretty good," she said.

"I'm not green anymore. I got broken in," I replied, before stepping back to study her in turn. Lindsey's skin was leathery and worn from the elements. Her clothing was a hodgepodge of different women's and men's pieces, all different sizes, put together to form an outfit.

I wanted to ask how she was doing, but she was living on the street. I found myself without words. I thought about telling her that I'd made my fortune in real estate, that I had a husband, a nice home, a kid, and a couple of dogs. But I couldn't.

Things got quiet, then Lindsey told me the reason I hadn't seen her anymore was because she had been removed from the foster home in our town. "I came home five minutes late one night, and the next day, I was told to leave for not following the rules." She lit a cigarette. "Their own kids were a half-hour late. I beat them home." Lindsey limped to a bench, where she sat down to rest as she continued with her story.

Foster care had been one bad home after another, and when she finally turned eighteen, she was told to move out, and quickly, to make room for another teenager. Her foster mom dropped her off in front of a shelter with a trash bag full of her belongings. She decided not to go into the shelter and tried to find a job, but one day she hid her belongings in a bush during an interview and they were stolen. At this point in the narrative, she started in a fit of coughing. I handed her my bottled water and waited as she gulped it down. When she was finished, she asked me if she could keep the water bottle to refill.

"Sure," I said. "Lindsey, I'm glad I got to see you again. I always wondered what happened to you. I got sent to a few foster homes too."

"Oh," she said. "I remember how much you liked the first one. What happened?"

"You know what, Lindsey," I said, "let me take you to lunch at a nice little restaurant I know, and I can tell you all about it. Maybe we can figure out how to help you."

After we reconnected, I was able to help Lindsey secure a job and find cheap housing. A few months later, when the trees started budding, reminding everyone that summer was just around the corner, she disappeared. Maybe it was too overwhelming for her to have new responsibilities, or she found something else, but I never saw her again. It was then that I decided that I wanted to give back to the community, to help those less fortunate. Mark and I opened a nonprofit organization and started organizing food and clothing drives for the homeless and helped a few secure jobs and homes. It put a fire in me and made me feel that I was giving back to the universe.

IN THE FALL OF 2016, I logged on to the computer to check the weather. I clicked *follow* on a news station website, so I could see daily updates about the weather and local news. Different stories flooded my screen. One story caught my eye. A man had sexually abused a child—one offense—and faced a prison sentence of between five and twenty-five years. I scrolled and read report after report of child sexual abuse, for what seemed like hours, until at some point it sunk in that my dad had gotten off scot-free for the things that he did to me. My mouth fell open at the realization. Dad had exposed himself to me, regularly, over an eight-year period. Why had he not served any jail time? I started researching more. There were thousands of cases, where the perpetrator served prison time for first offenses. I continued browsing on my computer when something flashed on my screen. It was the story of a movement that empowered women to speak up about sexual assault and harassment. It was called #MeToo.

The movement had gone viral.

I clicked on the hashtag and scrolled down, reading dozens of stories along the way. I felt that I could scroll forever through all the different testimonies—all sharing the same, horrible, common theme. I continued reading.

I remembered that day I first held Gabby, her warm breath on my cheek, tiny fingers curled around mine. It was our first pact as sisters. *We are in this thing together.* I was no longer alone. She needed me, though she didn't know it, but I needed her even more. I hadn't realized it at the time, but there is strength in numbers, even if that number is just two. My hand hovered over the mouse, before I started scrolling again and continued to read about the courage and power in the countless stories beaming from my screen. I was no longer alone. More than that—I never had been.

I VISITED THE POLICE station, where I was brought when I ran away from home at the age of fifteen and inquired about my case, which was now over a quarter of a century old. There was no record. I asked to speak to an investigator on duty. A man came out to meet me and walked me into an office, where another man sat half on a desk with his arms crossed. The investigator researched my case on the computer and came up with nothing. He said I wasn't investigated by their department because the actual crimes happened in another town. According to his research, an investigation was never done.

A great rush of emotion flooded me, in the form of a pain so sharp I could no longer stand. The man sitting half on the desk jumped up and grabbed my arm and guided me to a chair. My body was shaking all over.

I sobbed uncontrollably for several minutes. A box of tissues was brought into the room. I remembered speaking about the things that happened to me to a social worker, but no police officers ever came to speak to me. The truth was hard to swallow, and that truth was this: I'd been denied justice. As a teenager, I had wanted to testify, to be brave, but had been denied that privilege. Instead, I'd been smashed down, my fortitude whisked away by the wind.

Eventually, I composed myself and stood up. I wondered why no investigation had ever been done. Then I remembered that the man who would have done the investigation lived across the street from my parents. My dad delivered his packages.

———

MARK AND I CONTINUED flipping homes and running the mobile home park we owned. We bought dozens of mobile homes to rent out. By my mid-thirties, we were worth several million dollars in real-estate assets. We kept no cash and just enough money in the bank to buy more real estate. After my son left for college, we stopped taking in foster children, and I found myself getting restless with my day-to-day activities. When I went for a swim in our pool, it felt as pointless as if I were just hanging out in a large hole in the ground, and no amount of swimming could change that feeling. Grocery shopping became a mundane task, so my husband and I started eating out, almost daily. I couldn't stand to be boxed in my home any longer. I needed to get out and see the world, needed to be more a part of it than I currently was.

I could no longer stay still, so I found myself walking more often. I rose in the mornings, before the birds even started to trill, and I'd sneak past my sleeping husband into my closet for a pair of walking shoes, stuffed so full of small slips of paper that I had trouble lacing them up. I had slips for Dillon, Mark, each of my foster children, and countless other people in my life, as well as those who no longer were. I'd walk for miles, desperate to figure out what the next season in my life would hold. By the time I'd return home, ready to drop from exhaustion, I'd be certain that there had to be more purpose for me in life.

To lift my spirits, on our twenty-fifth wedding anniversary, Mark surprised me with a new car. We drove it to Baton Rouge and back. We were weaving in traffic when he suggested a place to eat. I agreed. He began telling me stories of things he'd done as a boy, most of which usually ended up with a broken bone. We were holding our sides with laughter by the time we ordered our food. The day seemed to transform me, pull me out of my funk.

My phone dinged. I didn't check the text. It was probably a tenant. Then it dinged again. And again. I checked my phone and saw that my son had texted, so had a tenant, but there was a text from one more person, someone I hadn't talked to in years: Amy.

―――

WE SAW EACH OTHER every few years and had exchanged numbers, though she rarely called me. "Please come get me," she wailed. "My boyfriend has been beating me and the cops are here. I just need to leave and go someplace safe."

"Where are you? Can you text me the address?"

"Why don't you just write it down?"

"I don't have a pen. I'm at a restaurant. Can you text it?"

"No, I don't want to text it. Find a pen and write it down."

I spent several minutes searching for a pen, then I drove Mark back home and put the address that I had written down into my GPS. I drove for over thirty minutes, before I turned onto a beaten-up road with so many potholes, there was almost no road left. I drove down it slowly, trying not to damage my car. Police units lit up the end of the road.

There were different rust-stained appliances and gutted cars scattered all over the bald yard. Several mutts barked in my direction. Amy stood outside amid the chaos, trembling.

Her bleached hair was matted with dried blood and dirt and bunched up, like a rat's nest in the back. Her eyes were still bright, but dark bags drooped underneath. She stood with lips taut and firm, her arms crossed over her chest. She didn't seem like the same Amy from thirty years earlier, who had flaunted Guess jeans, a fresh perm, and told me I needed a fashion consultant. She reached out to me now, in a ripped shirt, pajama bottoms, and camouflage shoes. As I put my arms around her, tears ran down her face. I knew she'd just realized she was now homeless.

An officer motioned to Amy that she needed to go into the house and pack her things. Wooden pallets were lined up to make a sidewalk through the mud. She marched across them, with her arms still crossed. After a few minutes, the officer returned outside and said that she was refusing to pack and that I needed to go talk some sense into her.

I cautiously stepped up onto a pallet and followed slowly behind the officer, careful not to fall through one of the slats. The inside of the house was filthy, and the smell of animal urine was so strong it made my eyes water. Wood shavings and animal feces were scattered on the floor. I walked past a room with a caved-in ceiling. Old furniture and trash were tossed about in there, like some sort of indoor landfill. Different shelves throughout the home were sagging and weighed down from hoarded items. Live animals—some exotic—peered through glass and wire cages. It was like a puppy mill for different species of animals, and Amy lived amid it.

In the bedroom, a pair of prairie dogs in a small cage stood up on their hind legs and watched the scene in the room unfold. Amy sat on the unmade bed staring into a wall, her arms crossed, and lips pursed.

"Amy, what's the problem?" I asked.

"My boyfriend said I could take my computer. How does he get to tell me that?"

The officer, who was growing impatient, said, "He is just telling you that it's yours, and you can take it."

"Oh, that's great, let's give him all of the power."

"Amy," I said, "just take the computer, and let's go."

"Whose side are you on?"

"I'm on the side that wants to go. Get your computer."

"He can't tell me what I can take and can't take. He's not my boss."

"Look," the officer said, "you need to pick it up and put it in the car."

"I'm not letting him win."

I was growing impatient. "I drove all of the way over here, down a road filled with potholes in my brand-new car to pick you up. You have ten minutes to have everything loaded, or I'm leaving without you."

She turned and looked at me, her eyes piercing into me, and said, "You are awfully bossy."

The officer was getting agitated. "Your friend drove all the way over here to pick you up, and this is how you are going to treat her?"

Amy stared at the officer momentarily, before saying, "You don't know anything. She's my foster sister. You don't know anything about foster care and what I had to go through." She then carried on a ten-minute rant about foster care before I interrupted and said I was leaving. The officer said she was being evicted tomorrow anyway.

In response to that she cried, "Well, then stop standing around and carry my stuff to the car. That's what y'all get paid to do. Not just stand around supervising."

The officer reached for his cuffs. I screamed at Amy to get her butt off the bed and help with her stuff. She responded by telling me I could already have had half the stuff loaded, instead of standing around too.

"Just help me and let's go."

It took us about half an hour to lug all her things into my vehicle. Amy kept trying to squeeze and smash her things in, and I'd say, "Hey, be careful, this is a new car." After the third time I said it, Amy shouted, "Yes, Tracie, we all know that you have a new car. You don't have to keep bragging about it!"

After I brought her to a hotel and helped her unload her things into the room, she told me that she was hungry. There was a taco place still open around the corner, so I told her I would bring her to get some food. When we pulled onto the road, she noticed that her knee was bleeding.

"Hang on," I said as I pulled the car over into a parking lot. "I have a roll of paper towels in the back. I don't want to get blood on the seat of my n—"

"Yes, I know," she replied. "Your new car."

I got out and opened the back passenger door. The paper towels were on the floor. I reached down and picked them up. Suddenly, a roach lunged at me from inside the roll. I flung it into the parking lot and looked in the back of my car. Roaches were scuttling everywhere. I didn't say anything, at first, to Amy, but got back in the car and drove as quickly as I could to the taco place.

After we made it back to the hotel with her order, she asked me to sit down. "No, I have things to do," I said abruptly, trying not to sound angry, but it didn't get past her.

"What's wrong with you?"

"Did your boyfriend have roaches at his house?"

"Oh, yes, he was infested with them. Thousands of them."

"Great," I mumbled. "Look, I have to go. Call me tomorrow."

I gunned it out of the parking lot, smacking at my legs as I drove, terrified that the roaches would crawl up on me. I ran into a twenty-four-hour store and loaded up on roach motels and roach spray. After I checked out and went back to my car, I opened all the doors and sprayed the inside. Then

I ripped the boxes of roach motels open and started tossing them randomly inside of the car. I waited for it to air out, and each time a roach faltered out of an open door, I ran to smash it. People stared at me and my can of spray as they walked into the store. A manager walked out and puffed on a cigarette as he watched for a few minutes. He probably figured I was just part of the usual midnight traffic of people, as he stomped his cigarette out and went back into the store.

I paced back and forth in the parking lot while the roach spray settled. My new car was now a giant scratched-up roach motel. I started to wonder if helping Amy was the right thing for me to do. Deep down, I knew that it was, and I stared at my car and remembered that it was just a car. Amy was a person—with roaches in tow, yes, but still a person. I waited for about half an hour in the parking lot before I closed all the doors and headed home.

I STAYED IN TOUCH with Amy every day, but I knew that she only had a few hundred dollars to her name from a cashed-out life insurance policy. I told her that she needed to find a women's shelter to go to, before she ran out of money. After a few days of phone calls, she found one. We got a mutual friend to help move her things to the shelter. Initially, she did well there and started searching for a job. But a few weeks later, she called me around midnight, telling me that she had been kicked out of the shelter. I got out of bed and drove there to pick her up. She was sitting on a dark curb, smoking a cigarette. The gate to the shelter was locked shut.

I edged my car up to the curb as she flicked the remainder of her cigarette into the grass and climbed in. Right away, she started grumbling about the shelter and how her roommate had wanted her to go to bed too early.

"Amy, it's after midnight, where do you want to go?"

"My roommate shouldn't have been online searching for a date. She's already had five husbands."

"It's really late. Where should I bring you?"

"I told her she should stop dating people. Five husbands are five too many."

I shifted the car into drive and started rolling toward the interstate. "I can either bring you to a hotel with what money you have left, or I can bring you to a vacant rental house that I have, but there is no furniture."

Amy crossed her arms and continued rambling about the roommate she had been arguing with all evening. After five minutes of this, I pulled over to the side of the road and told her that she had to decide. She looked at me and continued talking about the roommate and her five husbands. After several more minutes of her going on and on about nothing that mattered, I slammed my hands down on the steering wheel and screamed, *"I need a decision!"*

She looked at me and said that her roommate got to do whatever she wanted to do.

I shifted my car into drive once more and veered onto the interstate. Ten minutes later, we pulled up to a twenty-four-hour store. I told her we would purchase her an inflatable mattress and air pump and for the time being she could stay in my rental house.

She followed me into the store but got distracted by small vegetable trays on display. She spent fifteen minutes trying to pick out the perfect tray to snack on. It took nearly forty-five minutes to get the air pump and mattress purchased, because Amy kept getting distracted by different things. As we were walking past all of the empty registers to leave the store, she opened up the vegetable tray, stopped by a register, and started eating.

"Amy, what are you doing?"

"I'm hungry."

"I'm tired. Let's go."

"You are way too bossy," she said as she dipped a baby carrot into a small canister of dressing. "Anyway, I don't want to eat in your new car." She continued munching on vegetables, until I finally told her I was leaving her. She huffed and followed me to my car.

It was after two in the morning when I got Amy to the rental. I told her to air up the mattress, while I cleaned up some, but she said she didn't know how. She sat on the floor to finish eating the vegetable tray as she continued talking about the roommate and her five husbands. I plugged the air pump into the wall and hooked it up to mattress. It slowly inflated; once it filled, I told Amy that I had to go.

"But I haven't finished telling you about my roommate's husbands," she said.

I ran out of the door waving. "I'll hear about them tomorrow."

She waved back, ranch dressing dripping down her hand.

AMY TOLD ME THAT she had gotten a job at a restaurant as a server. I drove her to different department stores so she could purchase items for her uniform—white shirts, black pants, nonslip shoes, and black socks. She didn't have a car, so I had to bring her to and from work every day, grocery shopping, and for a pack of cigarettes every couple of days.

Little by little, Amy started making improvements in her life. After a couple of months, she found a room for rent, started buying little things for herself, and became independent. She thanked me repeatedly, saying that I was the first person who helped her all the way through, not just in the beginning. "You didn't just drop me and run. You pulled me up off the curb and walked with me, until you saw that I was going to be okay." She also told me that she had always been a little scared that I would come back, seeking revenge for all the things she had done to me.

I explained to her that I hadn't made it as far as I did to let a teenage Amy hold me down, or anyone from my past. "That was when we were young and weak. This is who we are now," I explained.

At first, Mark didn't understand why I was helping Amy, after everything she had done to me, considering how she had never been there for me. I couldn't explain it to myself, much less to him, but I felt like I was stronger than Amy, and I couldn't in good conscience leave her wallowing on the ground. I had to pick her up and at least give her a chance. It didn't matter that when I'd needed her, she wasn't there. What mattered, was that now, I needed to be there for her.

A few weeks later, Amy got fired from her job.

She soon found another job at a newly opened restaurant, but the tips were barely enough to cover the gas to get to and from work. I told her she needed to get a salaried job, within walking distance, but she said that she didn't want to go backward in life. I raised my eyebrows. She said she needed money for a card to serve alcohol. I gave her that, but the tips were still small, so she stopped going to work.

One day, she lost her driver's license and couldn't look for another job, because she had flags on the one that she lost. "How much do you owe?" I asked.

She shrugged. "I don't know. A thousand dollars or something."

"We need to get this taken care of, but I'm not loaning you a thousand dollars," I said.

"I'm more worried about the warrants. I probably should take care of those first. The cops are looking for me."

"How many warrants do you have?" I asked.

She started counting on her fingers. "Four."

"Okay," I agreed. "Let's see about those first."

I made a few calls and found out she was going to have to serve time for the warrants because she was considered a fugitive. It was agreed that she would voluntarily turn herself in. Someone else she knew said he would bring her to the jail to be admitted, and we could bail her out after. Once she was in jail, however, the judge refused bail because she had three fugitive warrants. Within weeks, she was shackled and loaded on a bus, and shipped to a prison four hours away.

Each morning followed the same pattern. I'd dial a judge's number at the courthouse, talk to multiple receptionists, secretaries, or temps, then they'd switch me over to someone else. I'd beg for leniency for Amy, then get put on hold or told there were other charges or fines elsewhere. I was afraid: Amy's trumped-up charges were stretched out over so many parishes, and the judges seemed so adamant about denying her bail, it looked as if she might not get out at all.

―

IN MID-DECEMBER, ALMOST four months later, the judge reduced her sentence and said she could be released. I was told it would be several hours, possibly the next day, before all the paperwork would be done.

It was late evening when I got the call to pick Amy up from jail. "She will be about another hour," the voice on the phone told me.

I left home with plenty of time, so I drove through the center of town. Train gates began to lower when I neared a railroad track. I steered into a parking space so I could stand and watch the train pass. It was starting to drizzle, so I pulled my umbrella out and leaned against the front of my car as the train blazed in front of me.

I pictured my brother, Bubba, whom I hadn't talked to in over a decade, playing with his trains at the age of seven. We often played with his toy trains together, connecting and reconfiguring the tracks. Trains always reminded me how I had left him behind when I ran away from home. I still had sort of a survivor's guilt. Though he had survived, he had not thrived. Decades later, I still felt bad for it.

I imagined that the trains were trying to tell me that, somehow, my life was off track. Something needed to be reconnected. Maybe that's why I was on my way to pick up part of my past. To fix what had been undone.

I felt that I had hurt my mother by coming forth with what my dad did to me—even though she hadn't believed me. Plus, not only had I hurt my brother by leaving him behind, but I'd also left my sister—the same sister I had promised when she was an infant to always be there for her.

I had believed that my family would always be a part of my life. In my twenties, I had carefully carved and sculpted them back into my everyday life. When I was finished, I stood back to breathe in and admire what I had accomplished, but the abstract form hardened into stone. They had become a solid obstacle, instead of a comfort or support. In the end, I walked away on my own terms, away from the drama and chaos, the backbiting and backstabbing, the lingering power my father held, in defining who I was to any ear that would listen. *She's nuts*. I decided to love the cold stone from afar, like a relic in the background of my life. I could still love it, without being hurt by it.

I felt like I had too much anger in my heart. I had been dragging it along for decades now, like a ball chained to my ankle. The wind from the train blew my umbrella back, and I grinned as I thought of Wind Horse.

But feeling that breeze, letting the winds of change carry me to the next chapter of my life, I recognized that my journey was not over. I had to forgive my family for everything they did to me. Just like I'd forgiven Amy. Wind Horse was still guiding me. As the train thundered past and the earth quaked beneath my feet, I could almost hear his hooves pawing at the ground. I knew that I had decisions that needed to be made.

It was still cold and drizzling when I picked up Amy. The lobby was tiny, the size of a walk-in closet. There were several people waiting. One woman had tossed her wig onto an oak bench, so I stood instead of sitting. She finally said her head was chilly and put the wig back on, lopsided, and waved goodbye to everyone. A few minutes later, Amy was escorted into the room, and we hugged, then she shouted to everyone as she raised my arm, "This is my sister!" We walked outside, and I opened the umbrella for both of us to stand under. "Come on, it's time to go home." We walked, arm-in-arm, down the sidewalk.

One evening, a few months later, the phone rang. It was Amy. She seemed lonely and told me that I was the best sister she ever had, that I didn't judge her, but supported her. We talked for over an hour before she mentioned something that could have been a game-changer in my life, had she related it to me when we were teens, living with Kate and James. I listened to her recount the story as I flicked through a magazine about house decorating. She said that she was in the scheduling office the day the school counselor scheduled us in all the same classes together. Kate told the counselor that she wanted the two of us to spend as many minutes together as possible, to be in the same things, to build the same interests. She wanted us to bond, *to be real sisters*. Amy said that, in retrospect, it was a missed opportunity for us. The magazine slipped to floor.

Usually, Amy had a habit of repeating herself when she spoke on the phone, so much so, that I often had to push her through to the next part, or on to another subject altogether. But not this time. She was blazing through the story, like a locust swarm moves through a field of wheat. Go back to what you said before, I told her again and again, but she refused. It's the past, she told me. I pressed my phone hard against my ear. I wanted more. There had been a great communication breakdown toward the end of my time with Kate and James. I listened to Amy's version about the class scheduling when we were young. I never questioned Kate. Amy called me a spy, part of a conspiracy to keep an eye on her in class and report back to our foster mom. We'd argued about it. I'd hated Kate for it because I believed it. How do you go back in time and ask questions, listen more? I wanted to slingshot myself thirty-five years into the past and hug Kate for what she had tried to accomplish, to tell her I was sorry for not trusting her. To try harder with Amy. I was only half listening while she steered the phone conversation in another direction.

As she spoke, my mind drifted in and out of a state of confusion. It felt as though I lifted a lid and opened Pandora's box. By doing so, my past and present were colliding like neutron stars, becoming something massive, a black hole, sending a ripple effect through the fabric of time. An intense desire chipped away at my brain, wanting out, wanting to go back and change things. I told Amy I was tired and had to go but didn't sleep that night. I couldn't. I lay in bed, piecing my teenage moments together with the new information Amy had shared with me. All those years ago, I misunderstood. Kate had not wanted me to supervise Amy. She wanted me to love her.

CHAPTER 23:

REFINED

While researching my past, I had to dig up all the old memories and abuses from the recesses of my mind. My first memory of my father is when I was four. He's target practicing with a pellet gun in our back yard. I'm the target. Mom hears my wails and scoops me up in her arms. It was also my first memory of her, saving me. I remind her of the incident twenty years later. She has no recollection. She said Bubba and I were always making up stories about Dad. Paranoid and obsessive, he clogs my memories as an enraged man with anxiety and low self-esteem. There *are* good memories of him, but they are so sporadic and far between, they degrade in the back of my mind, like radio signals do once they bounce off Earth into the atmosphere.

Before Gabby was born, I enjoyed my mother. She read books to Bubba and me and played board games with us. There seemed to be enough love in her for us. Every memory of Mom, after Gabby, is faded, compressed. Maybe my mother only had it in her to love one child deeply or spread the love equally between two children. I imagine her love as strawberry jam. There is only enough to fill one big jar or two small jars. I picture my brother and I both as open-topped vessels waiting to be filled. We wait for years. Our jars stay empty, but I look over and the big jar is full, overflowing. As a child, I had accepted the fact, that there was only enough love in my mom to give to Gabby. Maybe my jar was bigger than I thought it was. Maybe my mother's love could never fill the vast emptiness inside me.

I reached deep and started sorting the sexual abuses. There were so many, it quickly became an overwhelming task. So, I internally sorted them into bins by age and instance. Then, the bins started to multiply so quickly that I could no longer sort them by every instance. Sometimes, he crept into my room at night as many as ten times, so I began to figure the ten times a night as one instance. No matter how many times he came into my room in one night, I counted it as just one. Figuring it that way, over a span of eight years, between the ages of seven and fifteen, it still came out to over three hundred times. If I figured based on how many times he entered my bedroom door at night, it tallied to over two thousand.

Such a high number startled me at first, because I had never tried to calculate it before. One day, while I was driving my car and Mark was in the passenger seat, I asked him if he thought that three hundred times was a high number.

He stared at me as if I were crazy for asking and sighed, "Tracie, *one* time is a high number."

There were other things that I started putting together too. A few months after Mark and I got engaged, Dad told Mark not to marry me, that I was crazy. At the time, I was so used to Dad saying that about me that I hadn't given it too much thought. Suddenly, years later, it hit me. *He tried to keep Mark from marrying me.* He had been trying to sabotage me my entire life, because I had single-handedly fought him, since the age of seven. Because I wouldn't rip my clothes off for him as a child and because I had turned him in, he was going to make me pay for the rest of my life. Because when I was in the seventh grade, I had let him know he was wrong for sleeping with the fourteen-year-old girl who lived behind us, he would forever hold a grudge. At the age of eleven, I did not understand that he was committing statutory rape, and my family, *the same people he abused*, backed him, and called me crazy. By telling everyone I was nuts, he made me an unreliable source, thus making himself look like the victim—like *I* had wronged *him*.

As I thought about how Dad hadn't wanted me to be with a man who wasn't him, something familiar crept into my thoughts. My mind stretched back into the past, like a long arm, trying to thread the memories onto a projector. The reel clicked to life. I remembered my mother's screams of pain, my father's unmerciful beatings on her, time and time again, pounding her skull, cracking bone after bone in her body. That brought back childhood memories of *the men*. Men I never saw. Mark was one of the men Dad was afraid of. Dad wanted to be the only man in my mom's life and in mine.

I remembered how angry he got when my cousin Jack would visit our house with his girlfriend. Dad presented a different persona to Jack while he was there—smiling, laughing, jovial—but once he left, Dad screamed at Mom and beat her because Jack had come to visit. Jack was no longer a boy. He was a man. It didn't matter that Jack was my mom's flesh and blood.

When we were children, Dad kept us in fear, traumatized. Bubba and I had freedom to roam, but Mom had none. She lived in her own dungeon, one that only Dad had the key to. He put his kids on sentry day and night, watching. We had been foot soldiers in Dad's own personal battle with himself. His paranoia of other men had tugged the childhood right out of us, left both my brother and me stripped of any good memories of having been children.

Dad felt that all men were after his wife, and if all men were, surely that would include Mark—a handsome man whom I had to train not to sit, stand, or walk too close to my mother. It was the same story on repeat, but even more intensely so, because Dad was obsessed with me for reasons I will never understand. Maybe it was because I fought back. Maybe I didn't fight back hard enough. I don't know.

Because I had never put all these memories together, like the puzzle they are, I'd never realized just how sick my dad was. Now that all the parts of my life were unscrambled and interlocking inside my head, like steel pieces slamming together, I saw a full picture of who he was. It was obvious to me now, how he had trained all of us to backstab each other, so that he was the central character in charge of us.

My siblings and I never talked about what he did to us separately because he was always whispering in our ears about what the other ones said or did. We saw each other through the filtered lens Dad created for us. We never bothered to see if he was lying or telling the truth. I felt that I received the brunt of the sexual abuse, but I have no way of knowing who else, if anyone, suffered from it too. He instigated hate in our family to keep us from figuring out who he was. Separated people are easier to control than a unified group.

I wish I could speak to my father one last time, because these are the words I would say: *You will no longer tell my story. Your version of me will no longer hold precedence over my version. My voice will be louder and more powerful than yours. My story, for now and always, will be mine to tell, not yours.*

Dad, for the most part, got away with his crimes against me. Too many people bought into his rapturous personality and were slowly hypnotized into a narcotic stupor by his well-plotted web of lies. But the thing he never banked on was that his oldest child—who secretly had her shoes stuffed with hopes and dreams—would devise a plan of survival, fashion a weapon, parry his advances, and execute her own savage blows.

MY GREAT-GRANDFATHER WAS MURDERED when I was six months old.

I found this out last year after I took a DNA test. It was late winter when I opened my browser. A notice arrived in my email: *Your results are in.* My hand hovered over the mouse, unsure if I was ready to click. The white screen beamed me, a light ready to escort me to my past. I pressed my finger on the mouse and clicked. I began to research my ancestors by reading hundreds of documents available online: census reports, marriage licenses, birth, and death certificates. I found photos and dozens of articles about Grandma Avis's twin brother, Travis, who died in a high school boxing bout. There were photos of both of them next to each other in a high school yearbook, the same year he died. The next yearbook was just her, looking skeletal, worn. There were newspaper clippings about my paternal great-grandfather, Russell. He had arrests that were as long as my arm and stretched back to the 1920s. He was killed, months after I was born. There were articles about the murder.

I stayed on the internet long into the night, engrossed in the history that had been hidden from me my entire life. By midnight, I had so many tabs open, my computer froze. Early the next morning, I started researching again, constructing answers for odd or violent moments from my childhood: Dad's paranoia of men, trash bags covering our windows, the merciless beatings on my mother triggered by something as simple as a stale slice of bread. Fragments of my past churned in the corner of my mind. Memories, powerful enough to bring me to tears, surged in my brain with full force. There seemed to be a connection between Russell and my dad, but I couldn't put my finger on it.

I subscribed to a site online where I could view archived newspapers, old police reports. Russell was arrested dozens of times—not paying cab fare, theft, fighting, drunk and disorderly—over a period of forty years. But the arrests that stood out to me—and there were several—were for indecent behavior with juveniles. Doing further research, I found out those juveniles were his children, three boys and six girls. Throughout the arrests and court hearings, the children were sent away to live with relatives, or made wards of the state. His wife, Thelma, my great-grandmother, was a kind person, according to people who knew her. Russell beat her, sexually and physically abused the children, and she stood by him, like a rock, through it all.

The children suffered.

It felt like a thousand years since I'd talked to anyone from my family. Now a little tube of frothing spit had connected me to dozens of relatives I never knew existed.

I reached out to some, people I had never met, grilling them for answers. I found out that the men on my dad's side were womanizers. I heard more than one story of women or children being kicked across the ground by steel-toed boots. Time couldn't erase the past. My parents never mentioned any of the history that I learned through my DNA test. It was living and breathing through those who were alive, who lived it, and those who heard stories and cataloged them in their minds. Finally, after all these years—decades—my life began to make sense. The rage that exploded from my father, week after week, had been modeled after his own father, who modeled it after his.

One common thread I noticed in the women who endured abuses by their fathers was this: they had fought and struggled to be who they were today. As I spoke to woman after woman in my dad's line, I noticed they shared many qualities—confidence, wisdom, passion. But the quality that stood out to me the most, in the way they spoke of the past and the present and how far they had come, was strength.

The male children of that line grew up violent and angry, and handed those traits down to their sons, like an Olympic torch. One of those sons who became a torchbearer was my father. Dad was sent to a juvenile home around the age of fifteen. When he was released about a year later, his aunt and uncle on his mother's side took him under their wing, gave him a job in a funeral home they owned. He was to stay nights with the bodies of the deceased, guarding them and their valuables, such as jewelry or keepsakes. My mother, his girlfriend, took to visiting him at the funeral home on those lonely nights. His uncle did a surprise visit one evening and caught them in "compromised positions," as he later told anyone in town who would listen. He fired my dad on the spot. I was born almost nine months later.

My great-grandfather was known for spending time in seedy neighborhoods. He had a side girlfriend in one of these neighborhoods. Her husband came home and caught Russell sneaking out of his wife's bedroom window. A shot was fired.

A couple of days later, a car pulled up in front of Russell's home. It paused for a moment, then sped away. Thelma looked out the window.

Russell's body was on the front lawn.

———

I BEGAN RESEARCHING ON the internet about patterns or generational trauma. It was a hole as deep and winding as a rabbit's warren. It was late evening on the Fourth of July when I finally came across something that made sense to me. Fireworks were going off in the background, as if to celebrate my discovery.

It was called "repetition compulsion," a term coined by Sigmund Freud. All of us develop patterns over our lifetimes; however, some have been handed down for generations. People continue the patterns they see in their parents because it is familiar to them, comfortable.

I tried to understand why Dad blackened the windows when I was a child. He had carefully crafted our home into a dungeon, while making it still appear as a home. He monitored my mother's every second. My childhood had been foot-soldiering, keeping men I never saw at bay. I'd tried to understand a lot of things, but at the time, none of it made any sense. Now, after a lifetime, it finally did.

I continued testing my memories. I searched about men who were possessive. I typed in a few of Dad's symptoms: low self-esteem, extreme jealousy, fear of abandonment. The words borderline personality disorder floated across my screen. It was something I'd heard before. I read on with renewed enthusiasm. More words that triggered my past: explosive anger and out of touch with reality.

My mind drifted back to a memory I hadn't been able to erase. It lay dormant, relegated to the farthest point of my mind. When I realized what section of life my mind was traveling to, my entire body began to shake. Something inside me had awakened. My forehead suddenly felt hot. I stood up to fetch a glass of water, but I didn't make it as far as the kitchen. I couldn't go any further. The memory had pulsed to life. I crouched on the floor and dropped my face in my hands.

I was a teenage girl again, flicking through a book. Locked up. Dingy walls floated in my memory. Plastic seats. A nurse was speaking. *Maria!* She was talking about men who were paranoid, out of touch with reality.

Extremely violent. I'd looked up from the book. It had reminded me of Dad. Maria was explaining to a male patient that he showed the classic symptoms of borderline personality disorder. He'd denied it, of course.

Another memory took hold: Lena. She'd spent the entire summer and most of my seventh-grade year visiting my father on the weekends when Mom was at work. How he ended it had been odd. It was like a thorn that was stuck in the back of my mind. I couldn't pull it out, until then. I remembered that moment with startling clarity.

Lena and I caught a different bus for school at the same stop, around the same time, across the street from my house. She was in high school. One Friday morning, as we waited for our busses, her eyes kept drifting toward our house, then at the canopy of trees behind us. After a few minutes, a boy her age appeared at the edge of the woods. She grasped his hand and they disappeared in the trees.

I heard the screen door to our house slap hard. My head snapped in the direction of the noise. Dad burst onto the porch, jaw set, eyes blazing, searing the line of trees as he searched for Lena. Moments later, he stomped away. His pickup screeched out the driveway not long after.

The next day, Dad fetched me from the living room. He told me to tell Lena's grandfather, Mr. Gravely, that I saw her go into the woods with a boy. Mr. Gravely was outside, wearing a desperate expression. He wore a pair of denim overalls, like he always did. His hands were in his pockets. He anxiously looked to me for an answer.

"Go ahead, Tracie," Dad said. "Tell him what you told me, that you saw Lena go into the woods with a boy, instead of going to school."

I looked up at my father, pleading with my eyes for me not to be a part of this. Dad's face turned a deep red, sizzling ominously against the blue sky.

His eyes narrowed.

I turned toward Mr. Gravely.

"Yes, I saw them."

His face sank and paled so much it looked like it had been dusted with chalk. Dad slung an arm around Mr. Gravely's shoulders. "I'm here for you if you need me," he said. "But you need to send her where I told you. That's her only salvation."

I never saw Lena again, but I found out her grandparents had her sent her away, possibly to a detention home. I *think* that is what someone said when I asked about her later. In my memory, that person told me Lena was locked away in a detention home.

Even though I hadn't liked Lena for what she did to my mother, I knew what Dad did to her was wrong. On top of it, he'd flung me under the bus, as though I had been the snitch. Lena probably thought I was the one who told, and by Dad involving me in his revenge plot, I was.

It showed just one of the many patterns in my father's schemes. He had the uncanny ability to destroy girls and women, and he used that same ability to make himself look like a hero, when he was a villain. I had a feeling that his dad and his grandfather and perhaps others further down the ancestry line had been carbon copies of each other.

The rabbit hole snaked further.

On a hunch, I began pulling census reports, dating back to the 1700s on both my mom and dad's side of the family. I felt there must be a trigger point in our family's history. When did this evil begin? On my mother's side, it was a clean slate of people composed of constables, teachers, and small farmers. On my dad's side, it was much more complicated, but in a twist, their family seemed to have more money the further back in time the generations went. Neither of Dad's parents had much in the way of assets, almost nothing. I kept digging until I found a report that showed twenty-five people living at one residence, one of my dad's great-great-great grandfathers. *That's a lot of children*, I thought. But after reading the names and ages of the people living there, I realized they weren't the names of his children. My breath was tugged from my chest at the realization.

They were the names of his slaves.

As my eyes took in all the names, I wondered if this was where the snowball of hate began. Starting as a handful of snowflakes, thundering down a hill I was at the bottom of. I took a few steps back, and it had missed me.

The rabbit hole narrowed.

Perhaps this was the trigger point I was looking for. Could this person have passed down his hate for so many generations, onto everyone in his household? I discovered that trauma can also be passed down. People pass their hurt down, their pain. Generations of people, family, and slaves—hundreds or thousands of people—had probably suffered because of this one plantation owner.

This was all purely conjecture, but I was floored with the possibility. There were 46,000 plantations at one point in United States history. Every one of them, passing down a legacy of hate and trauma in some fashion. I wasn't sure if this was the trigger point that I was looking for, but I found all I needed to know.

I'd already figured that my father was a byproduct of possibly hundreds of years of hate and trauma, an atomic bomb of mental illness. Growing up, I hadn't known I needed an answer. But now, looking at the words that floated off the screen, I understood. There was nothing wrong with me. There never had been. I hadn't understood then, but I understood now. My dad was a broken person.

I realized the moment I picked up a pencil at the age of eight and tried to rewrite my future, placing it in my sole, I had put the brakes on what my ancestors were trying to pass down to me. It seemed so small at the time, just a few words here and there, but ultimately—walking in faith—I had reengineered my destiny. I couldn't figure out why the women fared better than the men, why they seemed to be so much stronger, but I was ready to close the rabbit hole. I closed out the open tabs and logged off my computer.

ONE OF THE RELATIVES I met online mailed me a photograph of my father and his siblings standing next to Thelma and Russell. Dad is about thirteen in the photo, boyishly handsome with a muscular build. I studied it, trying to understand the people who were posing. Russell wore a wide-brimmed hat, and in all the photos I've seen of him, he's wearing a similar hat, looking eerily like images I'd seen of Al Capone and Machine Gun Kelly—mobsters from the early 1900s.

They couldn't have known the future when they took this photo in the late 1960s, but staring at it, I knew. A few years after the photo was taken, I was born, my dad having just gotten out of youth prison. Months after that, Russell was murdered. Decades after Russell's death, generations of people continue to struggle with the trauma he inflicted on his children.

I've studied the photograph, probably a dozen times, my father's childlike face, his grin. It's hard for me to picture him as the monster he metamorphosed into. Like me, he just wanted to be loved. My mother loved him. He broke her bones. She loved him. He punched her. She loved him. He flung knives at her. Like the men before him, he treated his wife like a possession, his children as objects.

I believe Dad knew there were no men. It was all about systematic control. He kept us in fear of him, terrorized our days and nights, to retain control of the hierarchy that dated back so many generations; there was no way to figure out when it started. The rest of us were at the bottom of the pecking order, while one man remained king of his tiny kingdom.

Some people tell me that I need to let my past stay buried, to let it rot and be consumed by the innards of the earth, digested along with rotting corpses and decaying trash. The problem is, one of those rotting corpses is the teenage me I left behind. People—specifically my dad—are still calling her a liar, still saying, "She is nuts." I never stood up for myself when I was younger because I never felt strong enough to stand up to Dad or the town folk who supported him. Now, I feel like I need to set her free.

I have to believe in that teenage girl. I have to believe in me. Back in those days, I had no way of knowing that forty years later, I would still be wandering on this bizarre journey, trying to straighten out the damage my father caused me. I had to believe in the story that would thrive and shape itself within me, not knowing what would unfold from the pages of who I was.

My whole life, I entertained myself with stories of others, real and imaginary, while my story was the one my father dictated: a narrative full of lies, violence, and negativity. I never realized that I could write the chapters of my own life, that my own say-so had just as much power as his did.

When I ran away from home, it never occurred to me that anyone would take my dad's word over mine. He was an alcoholic who beat his wife and two of his children. He cheated on his wife with a teenage girl, and when he broke up with that one, he became completely fixated on another. His own daughter. He'd abused me since the age of seven, but after his relationship with Lena ended, he became obsessed with his newly turned teen-age daughter. Not only did people believe his narrative, but they stood beside him and bullied her.

There are moments when I close my eyes and imagine my fifteen-year-old self, walking along on the tracks, away from the place I called home, carrying nothing more than journals and a shovel. I whisper into her ear to run faster, to catch that train, to never turn back. *Go West. Don't stop.* She became afraid and derailed her plans and for years; I resented her for that. That teenage girl was supposed to be brave, to finish the race that she trained to win.

She caved.

I realize I wouldn't be the same person I am today, had she not stopped. Maybe we are separate people, she and I. Walking in opposite directions. Different visions.

Martin Luther King, Jr. once said, "Let no man pull you low enough to hate him." I keep that phrase, written down on an index card and taped next to my computer. It took almost four decades for me to whisper into the universe that I forgive my family for how they treated me. How my father secretly abused me and then trashed me for reporting him, how my mother chose not to mother me, and how my siblings didn't stand at my side when I needed them to stand by me.

All the miles I walked in my life, every word written on a slip of paper, were moving me in the direction of this one creed: to forgive those who have wronged me. The single greatest gift I gave myself was to forgive everyone in my family. I forgave Dad for having a few loose screws, for terrorizing our family. I forgave him for all the lies he spread about me, and I forgave all the people who believed him.

This was the key that finally liberated me from a decades-old dungeon.

There were bad decisions made by the men on the paternal side of my family. They went to jail. Their bodies got tossed out of cars. Their children paid the price for their bad decisions. I often wonder how Thelma, my great-grandmother, came to choose between her husband and her children. How she allowed a fox in the henhouse with her baby chicks. How, in the end, she chose to pledge her allegiance to a fox, while her distressed chicks scattered. I imagine my great-grandfather—a wife-beater and child-molester—holding a gun near, exposing the chamber, and telling her to touch the trigger. I picture a fox, teeth bared, crimson dripping from its lower jaw, lurking unencumbered in the henhouse.

Then, Thelma turns away to watch the back door.

I remember how abandoned I felt when my mom chose her husband over me. I remember my hurt and pain, the heart-stretched longing to have her stand up for me and say, *"Don't you dare lay another finger on my daughter again. Don't you dare."*

The girl I left behind tiptoed through the innards of the earth and slipped away unnoticed. The woman has been purged by the world's fire and has now reclaimed her identity.

The girl is weak. The woman is strong.

I like to think that I'm a little more polished now than I was in my teens. Mature. It didn't come easy. My feet were put to the fire. I walked and ran and biked and leapt, until I didn't think I could go anymore. I'd believed that hope and faith would have gotten me through life without a hitch, but there was one thing I was lacking, something I had no clue what it was. It was something I never received as a child, and I never truly understood what it was until I'd been purged through life, until the flames of my soul belched in the air. It took me a lifetime of walking with words underneath my feet, but I finally learned how to love.

Once I realized what it was, the power of it, my life became full, stronger. Faith and hope are nothing compared to love. It became the forcefield to my shield and the swoosh of my sword. Amy recently told me, "I don't know what it is about you that makes a person feel so special." It broke my heart when she said this, because it made me think of my brother and sister, who I never had a chance to bond with, to listen to, to love.

Not long ago, I ran into someone who remembered me from high school. His eyes lit up. He was a year younger than me and an old friend of my brother. "Your brother was so funny," he told me. I grinned when he said this. Over the last ten years, several people used that word to describe Bubba. *Funny.* "And you," he continued, "were so smart. Everyone thought you would be a scientist or a doctor." *Smart.*

When I was younger, people would say my brother was funny, that I was smart, and my sister was cute. I never liked to be called smart because I didn't feel I was. During my high school years, I missed quite a bit of class because of my great dumbing-myself-down plot. In foster care, I missed roughly half of my classes and winged my way through graduation. People still call me smart because of the person I used to be. I'm a lot of things, but I'm no longer smart. I'm okay with that. I started out school in the top of my class, with the ability to be promoted up several grades. I ended my high school year in the bottom 10 percent of my graduating class.

Even with faded slices of hope in my shoes, there were times in my life when I didn't believe that life could be good. That it could be amazing. Had I known, I wouldn't have needed to have faith at all, especially faith in myself. I still don't know when one journey ends and another begins. They seem to all be seamlessly stitched together, like pieces of a quilt. At almost every phase in my life, I felt like I failed. That I was too flawed to move forward.

Flawed people have paths to forge. They are brave. Decisions have to be made. The earth has to rumble beneath their feet. The girl in me had a path to blaze, and she jumped over every obstacle, ran like the wind, and fought like the Devil to get to where she needed to be.

The moment she stepped on the rail at the age of fifteen, she was no longer a weak little girl hiding under layers of quilts. She was a new person, ready to wage war. But that girl wasn't ready, not really. The only weapon she had was hope. At first, she was just like a soft breeze passing through, but by the time she was finished, she was roaring through every hurdle like a human tornado.

That teenage girl will not be buried any longer. She is being liberated. The words of my father will no longer keep her down. There will always be people who stand behind my father and turn their backs on me, and to them I say: *That is where you belong. Behind him.*

My dad, with all his charisma and package-delivering smiles, tried to destroy me. But he couldn't. Not as long as I could reach back in time and remember the few heroes who helped me along the way, gave me a spot in their home, or gently nudged me in the right direction. Not as long as I could stuff my shoes full of dreams, lace my shoes, and walk for miles, praying for a way out.

I'm no longer that teenage girl who was afraid to come out of her shell, but a strong woman who wants to spotlight and lay bare the evils of the world, the ones that prey on children. I want to move forward and be a change in the world. At the age of fifty, I understand that we are shaped by our ancestors but have the power to refine our futures into something beautiful.

My soul has been processed, cleansed, and purged from the impurities that tried to hold me back. My husband often tells me there is a reason I spent so much time playing around a refinery when other children were safe at home with their families. Maybe it was setting the stage for the rest of my life. He told me that *purged* isn't a strong enough word for everything I've been through to describe the person I've become.

The word he chose best describes what I am now: refined.

ABOUT THE AUTHOR

Tracie Breaux was born in Louisiana in 1971. She is the founder of *The Cash Queen*, a financial blog that empowers women to be financially independent. Breaux currently resides in Louisiana. *Refined* is her first book.

traciebreaux.com

Facebook.com/TracieBreauxLit

Twitter: @traciebreaux

Instagram.com/traciebreaux

Tiktok.com/@traciebreaux

www.ingramcontent.com/pod-product-compliance
Lightning Source LLC
Chambersburg PA
CBHW051827160426
43209CB00033B/1949/J